OPEN HANDS

*A Journey to Trusting the Lord with
Your Desires and Disappointments*

BY HANNAH PETTEFER

©2024 by Hannah Pettefer
Published by hope*books
2217 Matthews Township Pkwy
Suite D302
Matthews, NC 28105
www.hopebooks.com

hope*books is a division of hope*media

Printed in the United States of America by hope*books

First paperback edition.
Paperback ISBN: 979-8-89185-024-8
Hardcover ISBN: 979-8-89185-025-5
Ebook ISBN: 979-8-89185-026-2
Library of Congress Number: 2023921117
All Bible references use the English Standard Version unless otherwise stated.

Scripture quotations marked ESV are from the Holy Bible, English Standard Version. Copyright © 2001 by Crossway Bibles, a division of Good News Publishers. Used by permission.

For my parents, who taught me to keep my plans in open hands through their lives and their words.

TABLE OF CONTENTS

INTRODUCTION

I trust the Lord;
help me trust Him more.
I trust the Lord;
what does that mean?
I trust the Lord;
in all my inability,
I trust the Lord.

I look back on my life, and I see an innate need to control. To grasp. To know. My daydreams focused on excelling in my career rather than getting married because I thought I could control my career more than I could control falling in love. I was so determined to do well in school that I sacrificed my social life. I prided myself on my spiritual discipline and ability to perform. It's not like I didn't want more. I dreamed of marriage, spontaneity, and spiritual depth, but I didn't risk disappointment, so I didn't dare to dream it. Instead, I clutched tightly to what I thought I could control.

I look around me and see post after post and have conversation after conversation where we are all struggling to figure out how to hold our dreams, disappointments, and disasters. And while I and others may not recognize that this is a trust issue, it is.

We close our hands around what we think is best and cling to that for dear life. We grasp for these strong desires in our hearts—dreams of belonging, succeeding, or fulfilling. We wrestle with the disappointments that life throws our way again and again. We are burdened with disasters that disrupt everything, things beyond our control that we still long to reign in, understand, and manipulate. We plan and prepare our lives to meet our goals and fulfill our desires, but we are hurrying around when our Savior invites us instead to sit down, open up those hands, and trust.

We are called to keep our plans in open hands.

However, I find that most of the time, we don't open up our hands voluntarily. Quite often, something is ripped from our grasp, and we are left wondering how to pick up the pieces of the life we once thought we controlled. Sometimes the only way for us to open our hands to the goodness and glory of the Lord is for God to pry open our little fingers from around the plans we once held dear.

Corrie Ten Boom said, "Hold everything in your hands lightly, otherwise it hurts when God pries your fingers open."[1]

When he pries up our fingers, it hurts. Trust me, this book is the fruit of a lot of prying in my life. For me, that looked like the pressure of years of self-imposed perfectionism, a breakup, an injury, and career instability all funneled into one season. It looked like me letting go of my own self-righteousness and needing to prove myself. It looked like a lot of sitting, praying, reading, and crying. That season sucked. It was humbling. However, I see now that that season of prying tilled the ground of my heart to make room for a garden.

Thus, here we are. This book is for those who face the disappointments of life, both big and small. This book is for those who aren't sure they can fully trust God. This book is for those who tell others to "trust the Lord" but don't really know what they are saying. This book is for the girl who almost cried at the grocery store because she couldn't find the sweetened condensed milk after a long day. This book is for my friends, to encourage their souls to cling to the Lord at all times. And this book is for me, to remind my soul the riches of trusting God.

---

1 Corrie Ten Boom, "Quote by Corrie Ten Boom," Bible Portal, last accessed July 16, 2023, https://bibleportal. com/bible-quote/hold-everything-in-your-hands-lightly-otherwise-it-hurts-when-god-pries-your-fingers-open.

So, before we go any further, I want to start this book with a prayer. Will you join me?

Heavenly Father, You are trustworthy. Right here in our struggle to trust You we declare it: You are trustworthy. Your plans are better. They are better than our attempts to organize our lives. Your plans are better than our five-year ideas or grasping at what should be. Your plan is glorious.

We confess that our hearts and lives are often busy worrying. We are concerned with gaining security, comfort, and love. Without even knowing it, we curl our little fingers around our lives, timelines, and hurt. We wave our fists in the air at life, but You tell us that it is best to keep our hands open, ready to receive Your goodness.

We long for You to meet us here. Will You meet us here? Take these words and this space and fill us with greater trust in You. Take my humble words and do Your will. Fill us with who You are and delight our weary souls. What was once heavy, make light. What man meant for evil, change to good. What was in us that is reluctant to trust You, make soft to Your touch.

This is my pleading, Lord. This is our prayer.

To him who is able to do far more abundantly that all we ask or imagine, to him be the glory in the church and in Christ Jesus throughout all generations forever and ever (Eph. 2:20-21). Amen.

<u>Trust</u>

Figuring out if we have a vague, if not wrong, view of trusting God

CHAPTER ONE

"Trust the Lord; He'll provide a Better Man"

The Misguided View of Trusting God

Wave after wave crashes over me.
I need a rescue—
someone to change the waves into still waters.

Wave after wave crashes over me.
I need a reason—
why I'm caught up in this storm alone.

Wave after wave crashes over me.
I need some reassurance—
a feeling that all will be all right.

Wave after wave crashes over me.
I have this Rock—
I stand on solid ground.

I don't date much, so when I finally brought a boy to church, it was a big deal. Ladies who never come up and talk to me said hi. People rejoiced in my rejoicing, in the seeming answer to my waiting. Being Facebookofficial is one thing but bringing a boy to church . . . prepare the wedding vows.

Just so, when that relationship ended, the church also came alongside me, but they didn't know how to handle this part. They didn't know how to handle me crying in the church kitchen after my friend's bridal shower. They didn't know how to handle the fear that God wouldn't take care of me. Heck, I didn't know how to handle it.

Post-breakup, so many people told me, "God's got someone better for you." Or, "This is just preparing you for the next man, the real one." "Trust God, He'll provide The One." I know people were just trying to comfort me, but it seemed like a cheap answer to a hard circumstance. Yet how often do I respond to people's hurt with, "Just trust God"?

What I've come to see is that when people say, "Trust God," I think they really mean, "I hope it all works out." However, "Trust God" and "It'll work out" are two completely different phrases. Trusting God should hold deep power and certainty, unrelated to whether the One walks into my life. Those comforting words are vague hopes at best and heretical statements at worst. They are weak dreams in a change of my circumstance rather than a firm confidence in the unchanging character of my God. They assume that I know what is best instead of sitting at the feet of He who *is* best. This is confidence in the actions of God, rather than in His character.

That's not it. I'm calling it.

There's a reason why we tend to respond to tough situations with "Trust the Lord" and "Pray about it." There's a reason why there are so many inspirational phrases that go something like, "Let go and let God." There's a reason why, when faced with distress of our own, we grasp for comfort in those sentiments.

In those situations, we are forced to recognize that we are small, and we long to be able to trust someone bigger than us. We yearn for the safety of a Protector, the embrace of a Father, and the assurance of a Ruler. We are *made* to trust the Lord. That's how it worked in the Garden of Eden as Adam and Eve walked in the ways of the Lord. They weren't calling the shots. They trusted God. They weren't controlling the outcomes. They trusted God. But as soon as Eve started doubting God and trusting herself more, sin entered the scene (Gen. 3:6).

Sin whispers many lies to our hearts, but one of those lies is that God isn't trustworthy with the situation at hand. Satan might not be so obvious as to tell us that God isn't trustworthy at *all*, but perhaps God isn't trustworthy with *this* particular relationship, *this* particular work struggle, or *this* particular thought pattern. He just might not be present and faithful right here, after the seventh failed pregnancy test this year. He might be too far off right here, at one in the morning the week before finals when the world is piling up on your narrow shoulders. It's too small. It's too big. It's too complicated. So, we take hold of that relationship, struggle, or thought, and we live in a way that is *not* trusting the Lord. We take a bite from the apple because *just maybe* the Lord doesn't have what is best for us in store. *Just maybe* we can trust ourselves more than Him on this one.

My friend, I am writing this to remind us both that there is *more*. Trusting the Lord is richer, more powerful, and more certain than you think. To trust the Lord is our created wiring, and we should seek to not only understand what it means but to know that when we truly trust the Lord, our entire lives are freed up to operate in confidence and hope. When we trust the Lord with every area of our lives, we align ourselves with how we are made. When we trust the Lord with all our hearts, we get to dwell in delight even amidst the disappointments. Trust isn't just for the circumstances in life that are difficult; trusting the Lord is for all times at all places and can extravagantly change your life.

I'm on a mission to spell out what it means to trust God and strip away all of the fluff that we often attach to that phrase. True trust in the Lord isn't a bumper sticker pep talk. It isn't vague. It isn't easy. It is unchanging and purposeful. It is specific, personal, and powerful.

But first, let's talk about what trust is *not*.

TRUST IS NOT AN OUTCOME

I was talking to an unsaved friend about trusting the Lord and asked her what that meant to her.

"It bothers me when people just think that they can 'pray about it' and it will all be fine," she replied. "That's not how it works."

She was on to something. Non-believers can see what we sometimes miss. They can see how "Trust God; He'll provide a better man" doesn't line up with reality.

Do you find yourself, when telling your heart to trust the Lord, thinking about how He will work it out in your favor? You'll get the hire, the healing, the husband. Things will work out favorably because the Lord is good and gives good gifts. Right?

It's true that the Lord gives good gifts, but we are called to trust the Giver, not the gifts (Matt. 7:11). We are called to let Him define what is good, not the world or our own hearts. We are called to trust His character, not what He does for us. Even when things are hard, we can *know* and *rest* in the goodness of His character and know that all things work for good (Rom. 8:28). (More on that later.)

Because what if you never get the hire, the healing, or the husband? Is God not good then? What if I'm left unmarried and without the career of my dreams? Is God not good then? By no means! His goodness is not limited to our success and failures. He defines goodness differently than we do, and sometimes that is hard. Sometimes that looks like difficult jobs, terminal illness, or a life of singleness, and **that does not make Him any less good.**

Psalm 146:3 says, "Put not your trust in princes, in a son of man, in whom there is no salvation." God instructs us here not to look to the solution to the problem but to look to Him. The author of the psalm could have needed allies (princes), and hoped that the Lord would work in that way, but instead of trusting in an external answer, he says, "Blessed is he whose help is the God of Jacob, whose hope is in the LORD his God, who made heaven and earth, the sea, and all that is in them., who keeps faith forever; who executes justice for the oppressed, who gives food to the hungry" (Ps. 146:5–7). The Psalmist is looking to who God is, not what he wants God to do.

This is in direct contrast with many church movements that seek to proclaim healing and success for those who trust in God. That idea teaches that if you only trust enough, then God will come through. Whereas it is good and necessary to desire things like healing and breakthroughs, we must be on guard that we don't start to worship the healing over the Healer. We must adore the Savior, not the saving. And we mustn't think that it is our ability to trust that does the saving.

To put our trust in an outcome is to discredit the ways God uses for good what man intends for evil (Gen. 50:20). To trust only in what God does for us is to miss out on who He is. To put our faith in the idea that things will all work out is to be blind to the powerful testimony of those who have gone before us whose lives never got to that desired resolution (Heb. 11:39-40). If trusting God means that things will work out, what do we say about Habakkuk? Jeremiah? Stephen? Paul? Their lives were difficult and did not work out in the end. Did they not trust God, too?

In his book *Don't Waste Your Life*, John Piper orients our hearts not around outcomes but around Christ: "Whatever makes us more and more able to enjoy making much of God is a mercy. For there is not greater joy than joy in the greatness of God. And if we must

13

suffer to see this and savor it most deeply, then suffering is a mercy."[2]

This dispels any notion that our trust is in the outcomes of our lives. Our trust is that God is good, merciful, and perfect. If disappointments, disasters, or dreams-come-true help us better realize this, **they are good.**

* * *

You may not think that you struggle with trusting the outcome, but in subtle ways, you might. It's in how we expect to always have money, food, and two vacations a year. It's in how we compare our lifestyles to others. It's in how we enter a new year with the expectation that the Lord is going to "do great things" but the mindset that those "great" things include our comfort, a lack of disturbances, and our ability to control our lives. It's in our expectations that trusting God with our singleness means He'll help us get married. It's in assuming that trusting God with our sickness means that it ends in complete healing.

Perhaps the truest test as to whether you are trusting in the outcome rather than the Savior is whether or not, in the face of failure, your faith is shaken.

---

2 John Piper, *Don't Waste Your Life* (Wheaton, IL: Crossway Books, 2018), 58.

When I was in eighth grade my dad sat my sisters and me down in the dining room and told us he was starting a church. I cried for hours because I knew that this would be an isolating, difficult task in the days ahead. I'm not proud of that response, but that's what happened.

Every day for two years, I dedicated myself to praying for this little church. I got on my knees next to my twin-sized bed and prayed. Specifically, I prayed for a few young girls to come alongside me in this journey. I was homeschooled already, so having a home church was rough sledding. I've never before or after prayed for something with such devotion and faith. Why wouldn't God want to bless my desire for community? Why wouldn't God bless my dad's church? It seemed like a prayer with a sure answer.

Two long, lonely years later, we closed that chapter and ended the church plant. It didn't grow. No girls my age came. It didn't do the great things that we hoped it would. By perhaps the world's standards *and* spiritual standards, we had failed. God appeared to have not shown up. The outcome was disappointing. It was hard to explain to people why the church didn't work because we didn't know. It was a heavy question in my mind even as we entered a new season in a different, healthy church that I now love.

In that closing chapter, our trust was exposed. Did we put our trust in a God who always makes church plants thrive, or did we put our trust in a God who is still working, even in disappointment? Would we blame God for leading us to a place we couldn't finish as we intended, or would we look for who He was revealing Himself to be in this time? Would we trust in God's answer, even if it was "no"? Would we wait for *His will* rather than the outcome we desired?

TRUST IS NOT A FEELING

Just as trust isn't an outcome, trust also isn't just a feeling of peace. We seek to trust the Lord because we want to *feel* better. We want assurance that something is happening for the good, even in the challenging and sometimes downright terrible situations in life. We long for that peace, confidence, and assurance, but if we're just looking for a feeling rather than a Lord, we will come up empty.

True trust in the Lord leads to peace beyond understanding (Phil. 4:7). The feeling follows obedience, but the greater reward isn't the feeling of peace but the enjoyment of the greatness of God. I don't want to trust the Lord in order to feel better about the ways things didn't work out—even non-believers seek that kind of comfort. I want to trust the Lord because through Him, I can behold His glory and be transformed (2 Cor. 4:18).

Trust isn't just feeling good about life. Trust is coming to God with all the ways you feel terrible about life and placing that in His hands. Yes, trust is an emotional response to life, but it is also a game of the mind, a choosing of the will. To trust God isn't just to feel good about the direction of your life but to press on to His goodness no matter what you feel.

Isaiah details how trusting God and feeling at peace work together: "You keep him in perfect peace whose mind is stayed on you, because He trusts in you. Trust in the LORD forever, for the LORD GOD is an everlasting rock" (Isa. 26:3-4). There is no drug-like feeling of peace that follows a decision to trust God. There is dedication of the mind and recollection of God's character. Then, God works perfect peace in our lives, not just happy feelings.

* * *

During the time when my dad planted his church, I was so lonely, and in the waiting, I didn't *feel* God at all. I'm usually a passionate person, and I love to be in tune with the Spirit and His fruit, but my eighth- and ninth-grade years were hard. They were what some people call a "dry season."

I'll never forget this moment, although it didn't seem memorable at the time. I was learning how to drive, my dad in the passenger seat. We were talking about faith and the church, and I mentioned how I kept praying for community and vibrancy to my faith only to come up empty. I felt numb to His kingdom. Was there something wrong?

Something clicked there as we passed the familiar neighborhoods on the way back home. I'm not sure if it was something my dad said or just the Spirit working in my mind, but I knew, *knew*, right then, that I trusted the Lord even if I didn't feel Him. I didn't need the feelings to confirm what I knew to be true.

I don't exaggerate when I say that this realization transformed my life. It brought me so much freedom because then I didn't have to freak out during the seasons of my life where my emotions were unreliable. When we trust in God with more than just a feeling, then we build a solid foundation upon the *truth*. We no longer have to be afraid of shriveling up in the dry seasons because our souls are planted by his living water (Ps. 1). We no longer have to question His goodness when we feel bad because we are established in His Word and confident in His character.

TRUST IS NOT AN ANSWER

Sometimes we view life like an episode of a Disney Channel show. There's a problem, there's a solution, and there's a neatly tied-up lesson at the end of the twenty-three minutes of screentime—a lesson we will likely forget during the next episode.

Life doesn't work that way. We don't always get the answer at the end of the episode, month, or season. Sometimes it takes years or lifetimes to understand why things happened. Perhaps we are too hasty to neatly piece together the lesson of the season. We get a certain satisfaction from knowing that it wasn't all for naught. We want to clearly label everything at the end of the season, but who are we to know how to label it, let alone know if the season is even over or not?

This isn't to say that we aren't to come to the Lord with our *whys*, but that we should, as Jerry Bridges says in his book, *Trusting God*, "Ask God to enable us to understand what He may be teaching us through a particular experience. But even here we must be careful that we are not seeking to satisfy our souls by finding some spiritual 'good' in the adversity. Rather we must trust God that He is working in the experience for our good even when we see no beneficial results."[3]

---

3 Jerry Bridges, *Trusting God* (Colorado Springs, CO: NavPress, 2016), 119-20.

God wastes **nothing.** There is a reason, a lesson, and a purpose behind all things in life. He is intentional to the utmost. But I'm hesitant to name His reasons too quickly. I'm hesitant to wrap up the season with a little bow and declare, "This is why this happened to me."

Isaiah makes clear that our understanding and ability to find answers are limited, anyway, when he says, "For as the heavens are higher than the earth, so are my [God's] ways higher than your ways and my thoughts than your thoughts" (Isa. 55:9). Isaiah also says, "Who has measured the Spirit of the Lord, or what man shows him his counsel? Who did he consult, and who made him understand?" (Isa. 40:13–14). We see in part now, without all the answers we desire, but we will one day see in full (1 Cor. 13:12).

* * *

I did ballet for twenty years, and with this territory comes certain risks, including breaking your feet. When I broke my foot for the second time, I really struggled with knowing the "why." After all, I had already broken my foot before. We had gone over this; I learned my lesson last time about putting my faith in my abilities and my identity in ballet. Why did I break my foot again? Although I knew God was at work, I couldn't tell you how.

People around me were eager to point out all the lessons to be learned and reasons why I broke my foot at what seemed me like the most inconvenient time. I was a senior in college, had four jobs, and I'd just started a character performing company consisting of . . . me. Last I'd checked, Cinderella's other slipper wasn't a walking boot. I wasn't having it. The "reasons" and "lessons" seemed like cheap ways out. They were add-ons to life's experiences, ways of making sense of things to me, but more of a filter than reality.

I wonder if, when we're hasty to put an answer to why things happen to us, we are trusting our ability to understand the circumstance rather than trusting in the One who holds all things together? I wonder why we try and shape things to make them fit our limited understanding when we should learn to take a step back and wait a minute. The Lord will make clear that which He desires.

Timothy Keller, in *Walking with God through Pain and Suffering,* says, "So we can trust him even when he hasn't shown us yet the reason why. He is good for it."[4]

I *did* see the Lord's mercy to me the second time I broke my foot, but I didn't grasp it until a year later.

---

4 Timothy Keller, *Walking with God through Pain and Suffering* (New York, NY: Penguin Books, 2013), 154.

The first time I broke my foot, it humbled my pride and relocated a bit of my confidence to the Lord. The second time I broke my foot, it literally forced me to slow down in what turned out to be the craziest, most stressful time of my life. If God hadn't forced me to sit down for two months (literally), I'm not sure I would have made it. And I'm still seeing how even something that small is shaping my days today. Even the lesson that not everything has a clear lesson is something He's using (see what I did there?).

*   *   *

So often we come to trusting the Lord for one of these three reasons—outcomes, feelings, or answers—and, not to contradict myself, that's actually okay. It's okay to come to the Lord needing to trust Him because we need to make sense of the world. We may come to Him needy, selfish, and small. We might just need comfort in the suffering and light in the darkness. But the Lord doesn't answer those needs with just an outcome, feeling, or answer. The Lord doesn't just give us a hug while we're in the mud of it—he places our feet on solid ground, making our steps secure (Ps. 40). The Lord leads our confused hearts to a sure truth, not a fleeting feeling, temporary outcome, or short-sided answer.

What is your tendency? Do you tend to come to the Lord for outcomes, feelings, or answers? Be honest here, and then, even in your need and inability, come. Bring all your mess and come. He is more than capable of taking our misguided views of trust and refining them to be more and more Christlike. He desires to guide us into a sure view of His trustworthiness.

My friend, I know that it is hard to trust the Lord. I know that our hearts desire things like outcomes, answers, and feelings, but let the Lord take your hand and lead you to spacious places. (Ps. 40). Let Him make a path in the wilderness and a river in the desert (Isa. 43:19).

GROWING ROOTS

▶ What outcomes do you want in life? How can you learn to trust God, whether or not those outcomes come to fruition?

▶ Do you search for answers, or do you rest in assurance that God is in control?

▶ How do you think your trust in God is in search of a feeling?

CHAPTER TWO

What is Trusting God?

How to Be Particular, Personal, and Powerful When We Say, "Trust God."

Trust isn't blind.
It sees the Cross and goes toward it anyway.

For a few months, I asked most everyone I met up with what it meant to them to trust the Lord. No fluff. No religious jargon. I wanted to know what they told themselves to think. I wanted to know how they felt about trusting God. I wanted to know what was beneath the surface of "just trust God" for them.

This simple question stumped some people. They had to ponder.

Some said that trusting the Lord was looking to His faithfulness in the past. *Very true.* Others pointed out that trusting the Lord is surrendering in the present. *Also true.* Still others said that trusting the Lord is about reorienting our priorities around the kingdom. *Still true.* (My friends have amazing hearts for the Lord that constantly encourage and inspire me!)

I, too, pondered. I pondered so much that I accidentally wrote the first draft of this book. I considered all the different ways people depicted trusting the Lord, I examined Scripture, and I prayed until I couldn't contain it anymore. Thus, this chapter came to be (and really, this book!).

A year ago, I would have said trusting the Lord is releasing the need to control the outcome, which is what many of my friends said. I thought of trust as a passive thought or waiting. I used to think trusting the Lord was a back-of-the-mind process, like a pot on the back burner.

Although I still see so much value in that way of trusting the Lord, I also see it as a battle. It's more like a tea kettle on the back burner than a pot, and if you haven't heard a tea kettle scream, you're missing out. The British have led us to believe that making tea is this peaceful, quiet endeavor. No, the kettle screams its little heart out when it's ready. Even if you leave it on the back burner, the kettle is not going to let you forget it.

The same is true of trust. We might put it on the back burner, but it is loud. It is not going to let us forget that we need the Lord. Trusting the Lord is actively redirecting our thoughts (2 Cor. 10:5) and extinguishing the flaming arrows of Satan's lies (Eph. 6:16). Trusting the Lord is ever putting His character in front of our vision so that we do not make the things of this world too important, too beautiful, or too urgent. Trusting the Lord is teaching our souls to sing in disappointment and disaster. Trusting the Lord is courageous.

It's not "just trust God," but "God is so trustworthy—look to Him!"

Perhaps the most familiar verse about trusting the Lord is Proverbs 3:5: "Trust in the LORD with all your heart and do not lean on your own understanding."

I tend to throw this verse around when trying circumstances arise but not sit in the depth of what it means. Let's investigate together.

TRUST

Trust: (Hebrew, *bāṭaḥ*) to trust, trust in, to have confidence, be confident, to be bold, to be secure (used 120 times in the Old Testament)[5]

The Hebrew definition of *trust* emphasizes **confidence.** Trust isn't a passive thing, something that

---

5 "Lexicon: Strong's H982: *bāṭaḥ*," Blue Letter Bible, 2023, https://www.blueletterbible.org/lexicon/h982/esv/wlc/0-1/

just happens on the back burner. It is confident and sure. Where does confidence come from, though, except from tested experience and knowledge? We aren't confident in something we don't *know,* unless of course it's false confidence. From the onset, we see that trusting the Lord has a lot to do with knowing the Lord.

However, in many ways, trust is like hope. There is an element of unfulfilled promises that you hope will become fulfilled. There is a part you currently have and a part that you expect to have. You may trust that the plane will land. You have the confidence of your past experiences, the quality of the vessel, and the statistics behind plane crashes. But you don't really *know.* You hope. There is an element of faith to trust, an element of hoping in something not yet received (Heb. 11:1). (My apologies to anyone with flying anxiety for that example.)

When we trust someone, we are, because of our confidence in their ability and assurance of their character, surrendering what we think is best to them. It's like riding shotgun. We get in the car with someone and have to *trust* that they can get us safely to where we want to go. We've surrendered our ability to control the outcome because we literally do not have the wheel.

IN THE LORD

When you put "trust" like that, it sounds scary. That's a lot of confidence. That's a strong assurance. How do we know it is safe? How can we trust this driver? I'm always one to prefer to hold the wheel with my own two hands before I let someone else drive.

We are not called to trust everything—indeed, we are called to trust nothing apart from the Lord. Thus, when defining trust, I must make a clarification that this kind of trust is reserved for the Lord. He is the only one who can handle it.

And, my friend, He can handle it.

Trust, then, is to get on the plane with the confidence that the plane is safe and not need to check it out for yourself. This only works, though, when you're flying with a tested airline with a licensed pilot and professional staff. Trust isn't to board an unknown vessel with a sketchy pilot with naïve confidence. It is to know who you are trusting and put it in their hands.

If our deepest trust, this firm faith, is to be in the Lord, then it is clear that we *must know who the Lord is*. We must come close to Him and know that He is trustworthy. We must draw near to Him and see that He is good. We must behold Him and wonder at His glory. We must spend time with Him and know that

He is sovereign. When people I know seek to trust the Lord with their disappointments but do not put value on *knowing the Lord* more and more, I see little fruit.

This is so important that we will spend the whole next chapter on it.

WITH ALL YOUR HEART

God is pretty extreme, isn't He? He doesn't just want a little bit of our trust, He wants it all. He doesn't just want a little bit of what's best for us, He wants it all. He doesn't just call us to kind of depend on Him, He wants to take away everything else that we leaned upon and be our sole, firm support.

When you get on a plane to fly somewhere, you are 100 percent on that plane. You can't just 50 percent take the plane and 50 percent take the drive to get somewhere. You sit your butt down in those stiff seats and trust that this plane is taking you to where you want to go.

God wants us to trust Him 100 percent.

This reminds me of the greatest commandment: "Hear, O Israel: The Lord our God, the Lord is one. And you shall love the Lord your God with all your heart and with all your soul and with all you mind and with all your strength" (Mark 12:29–30).

To love the Lord our God with all our hearts means to not hold within our hearts and hands love for other things. We cannot trust God some and trust ourselves the rest. We cannot love God with some of our heart and love money with the other part. We cannot hold our hands open to the Lord if we are still grasping for other sources of trust. Augustine says, "God is always trying to give good things to us, but our hands are too full to receive them."[6]

I teach ballet, and in my middle school class I constantly remind them that if they are going to be present in this dance studio, they might as well give it 100 percent of their effort. If not, it is a waste of their time and mine. They are physically in this space. They can't be doing something else. They might as well work hard, get better, and give it their all. Similarly, if we say that we trust God yet reserve some of our trust back, we are diluting our own time and effort.

AND DO NOT LEAN ON YOUR OWN UNDERSTANDING

All the ways that we tend to have vague trust in the Lord discussed in the first chapter are because we lean a little too much on our own understanding. We understand

---

6 Michael R. Heinlein, "St. Augustine of Hippo," Simply Catholic, Our Sunday Visitor, 2023, https://www.simplycatholic.com/st-augustine-of-hippo/.

outcomes. We understand answers. We understand desirable feelings. We understand that when we board a plane headed to Boston we will land in Boston.

What's difficult about trusting in the Lord is that He decides where it lands. We may have our ideas and expectations and desires, but trusting the Lord is to trust His map of the journey. It is an open-handed endeavor. It is surrendering our pride of thinking that perhaps we know better. It is laying aside everything that hinders and the sin that so easily entangles (Heb. 12:1).

This should *free* us, though, for our understanding is limited, selfish, and tainted. We can't see very far—only past our own noses. We certainly can't see years ahead or into the needs of others' hearts. We wouldn't fly to a place with only a pair of binoculars to guide us, so why would we trust ourselves to guide our lives with our puny perspectives when God sees the infinite? To trust the Lord with our destination isn't a grand sacrifice, it is a great reward. The place He is taking us is *best*.

Elizabeth Elliot said, "There will be those who can 'explain' to you God's purposes in all of this. They'll 'see' what it's supposed to mean for you. Don't worry about them. They are blind. No explanation this side of Heaven can possibly cover the data. It's imponderable, inexplicable, and far, far beyond any explanations. You have to cast all that nonsense on the Rock too."[7]

That doesn't mean that it isn't hard, though. Let's look at Abraham.

God made some big promises to Abraham. He promised Abraham land, wealth, and a nation. But perhaps the most specific promise and the one with the biggest emotional pull on Abraham and Sarah was the promise of a child. That promise wasn't just a bonus point for them but a core desire and deep longing.

I know you feel it, too. Everything could be going great, but there is perhaps one thing that is lacking, and that one thing has a lot of pull. Your career could be skyrocketing, but you don't have the community your heart longs for. Your ministry is growing, but your family still doesn't know the Lord. Your friendships are encouraging, but you still seek marriage. This one thing is the thing your hands long to grasp, but it always seems to slip through your fingers. For me, that struggle is marriage. I love my job, friends, and family. I have the life I worked hard for and dreamed about, but since I am unmarried, I feel this longing still.

---

7 Lisa Appelo, "50 Elizabeth Elliott Quotes on Suffering," Lisa Appelo, May 28, 2021, https://lisaappelo.com/ elisabeth-elliot-quotes-on-suffering/.

I imagine that for Abraham and Sarah, childlessness was the hardest thing for them to come to terms with in their lives. Sarah could have all the clothing and servants her heart desired, but her truer heart's desire was a child. Abraham could have all the donkeys and wealth he could accumulate, but who would he pass it down to if he didn't have an heir? We must also realize that childlessness was more important in Abraham's culture than ours. It was a great shame and logistical burden for bloodlines, inheritances, and growth of the culture.

Enter in God's promise: "Look toward heaven, and number the stars, if you are able to number them. . . So shall your offspring be" (Gen. 15:5).

God made a huge promise to Abraham and asked Abraham to *trust Him.*

We think of Abraham as a man of faith. He's the founder of Israel, after all, and in the Hall of Faith (Heb. 11). However, Abraham had many moments of distrust. He had many moments where he put his plans above the Lord's. He had many moments when he closed his hands around what he thought was best.

He acted with distrust in Egypt when he lied about his marriage to Sarah (Gen. 12:10-20) and again in Negev when he lied again about being married to Sarah (Gen. 20:1-18). He perceived real danger, but he stopped looking at the hands of God to provide and took things into his own hands. These incidents had real consequences, for in Egypt, the Pharoah and his household were afflicted with plagues until Sarah revealed herself to be Abraham's wife. In Negev, Abimelech suffered from some sort of illness and all the women of his household were childless until Abraham and Sarah walked in truth. The consequences of distrust affected more than just Abraham and Sarah; they affected entire households.

Then there's Hagar. Hagar was Sarah's maidservant (Gen. 16:1-4), and in the culture, if the mistress was barren, the master could sleep with the maidservant and the child would be considered his. After waiting and waiting for the promised son to come, Sarah and Abraham decided to help God out. They lost trust that God would come through. Maybe God was waiting on them to take things into their own hands. Maybe God had forgotten about them.

Nope. Ishmael was not the answer. In fact, Ishmael would in turn parent another bloodline, the Arab nations, who continue giving Israelite nations trouble to this day. The consequences to not trusting the Lord were yet again high, and Abraham and Sarah saw that.

What is so encouraging is that God didn't give up on Abraham just because Abraham acted out in distrust.

Instead, God drew near and reminded him that the promise was as good as done. Abraham just needed to wait, and this time God gave him a deadline. By this time next year, they would have a child.

Sarah laughed.

But a year later, she was holding her precious son in her arms. A year later, I imagine that every time Abraham looked at the night sky, his heart fluttered. God's promises are true. He is a trustworthy God indeed. The deep longings of their hearts were satisfied by the Lord's grace. The promises of a blessed nation seemed to be unfolding. They didn't even know that they had the gospel to look forward to, but that was coming too, through their son.

When Isaac was young, God called on Abraham again. "Take your son, your only son Isaac, whom you love, and go to the land of Moriah, and offer him there as a burnt offering on one of the mountains which I shall tell you" (Gen. 22:2).

Hold on a minute. That made no sense. After years and years of promising a child, time and time again foretelling that a nation will come from him, now the Lord was going to take the child away? More than that, He demanded that Abraham sacrifice his child? It made no sense.

They packed up early in the morning and Abraham busied himself with the preparations. Some may credit him with a calm trust, but I doubt Abraham was calm. I venture to say that everything in him was screaming how this wasn't right. He couldn't do it. Why would God ask this of him? After all this time, the precious gift of a son was in his hands, and Abraham wanted to hold onto that gift tightly. The promises that God made were directed towards Isaac. How could this be God's plan?

Perhaps Abraham remembered the times when he took things into his own hands and how it *never* worked out. Perhaps Abraham knew that God gave Isaac to him, and his son wasn't his own. Perhaps Abraham had a gut feeling that the Lord would work it all out in his favor.

Perhaps, though, Abraham knew none of this and simply trusted the Lord with the questions, hurt, fear, and desire to control. Perhaps Abraham's story is the most extreme example of someone leaning not at all on their own understanding but trusting in the Lord with all of their heart, and all of their son's heart, too. Abraham's understanding would have yelled at him that this wasn't it. God had said that Isaac was the promised one. It wasn't right to sacrifice your child. Abraham, though, leaned on the Lord's word over his understanding, even his understanding of the Lord's word. Perhaps this is truly keeping our plans in open hands, for Abraham put it all—all his confidence, dreams, and fears—in open hands and trusted the Lord in obedience.

Hebrews elaborates on this gutsy trust: "He [Abraham] considered that God was able even to raise him from the dead, from which, figuratively speaking, he did receive him back" (Heb. 11:19).

I wonder if Abraham looked up at the stars on the three-day journey towards his son's sacrifice. I wonder if he saw the evidence of the Lord's faithfulness. Because I can think of no other way that Abraham could do what he did aside from the fact that he trusted in who God was, not in what God would give him. Abraham trusted that God was a faithful God, not that God would faithfully give him all that he wanted. Abraham trusted that God was a powerful God, not that God would work in power to remove every obstacle from his life. Abraham trusted that God was merciful, not just that Abraham would understand the workings of this mercy.

Then the moment came, and we all hold our breath to see if this is true trust in the Lord or if Abraham was just putting on a show. Was he really trusting God or was he just biding time, waiting for the Lord to tell him what the heck was going on? Abraham prepared the altar. He tied up Isaac. He placed his dear son of the promise on the altar. He raised the knife. There wasn't a moment to spare here. God really drove home the reality that Abraham would have done it. Abraham gave up his understanding and walked by faith in God *no matter what.*

> But the angel of the LORD called to him from heaven and said, "Abraham, Abraham!" And he said, "Here I am." He said, "Do not lay your hand on the boy or do anything to him, for now I know that you fear God, seeing you have not withheld your son, your only son, from me." And Abraham lifted up his eyes and looked, and behold, behind him was a ram, caught in a thicket by his horns. And Abraham went and took the ram and offered it up as a burnt offering instead of his son. So Abraham called the name of that place, "The Lord will provide"; as it is said to this day, "On the mount of the LORD it shall be provided."
>
> —GENESIS 22:11-14

Exhale. The Lord provided. He was trustworthy again and again.

Some speculate that Mount Moriah is also Calvary, and whereas I don't see enough evidence to back that exact theory up, the story of Abraham/Isaac and God/Christ are mirrored. I don't know about you, but the heavy demands of God in Abraham's story can be hard to puzzle together. Child sacrifice is heavy and doesn't seem in character with God at all. I get that we're supposed to trust the Lord with all our heart and lean not on our own understanding, but if it means *this,* I'm not sure I'm in. We may think that about our own lives, as well. We get that we're supposed to trust the Lord in all things but if it means [insert terrible situation], we're not sure we're in. I trust the Lord, but if that means a life of singleness, I'm not sure.

You see, though, there's a gospel-sized hole in the story of Abraham and Isaac. Their story won't make sense until we see that *God* bound up His own Son in human flesh and prepared His Only Son's altar, a wooden cross. The Son climbed up the mountain, the altar tied on His back. We won't understand why Abraham had to be so open-handed about his promised son until we see God's Promised One with hands outstretched on the cross. The point of Abraham's story isn't so that we trust God because He always provides. The point of Abraham's story is the gospel. God is making a way of provision, but it's not about our circumstances; it's about our hearts. From the beginning, God is after the redemption of our souls, no matter the cost.

On the mount of the Lord, it was provided. It was finished. And that, my dear friends, is our confidence to trust the Lord and lean not on our own understanding. The story of Abraham, in all his mistakes and triumphs, points our souls to trust in who God is, and the gospel gives us open eyes to see who He is. For if the gospel wasn't true, this story would be a mean tease from God. If God didn't sacrifice His Son, then Abraham's trust would have been an extreme trust agility exercise from a cruel trainer. But the gospel *is* true. The Son of God really *did* come and die for us. And in light of the gospel, we have eyes to see a God who held nothing back in pursuit of His children, not even His own Son.

I'll never understand that kind of sacrifice, and *that* is why I trust God and lean not on my own understanding.

GROWING ROOTS

▶ What do you mean when you say that you trust the Lord?

▶ What are ways you lean on your own understanding?

▶ Where do you find encouragement of God's faithfulness?

CHAPTER THREE

Is God Trustworthy?

Who Are We Even Trusting?

He doesn't respond to my cries with a
Process,
Purpose,
Or Proposal.
He gives me a Person,
Himself.

He doesn't answer my question with a
Textbook,
Tease,
Or Tactic.
He sings a love song over me,
Because that is Who He Is.

I often struggle with decision fatigue. For example, when I'm choosing a cookie recipe and search "Double Chocolate Cookie" on Pinterest, the options often paralyze me, and I lose my desire to bake. If I'm searching for skin care recommendations, I see too many people recommending too many options and usually don't buy anything.

However, this all changes when I find *my people*. Once I find a food blogger who creates clear recipes that I enjoy consistently, I forgo Pinterest altogether and simply look to her site. Once I establish a friend who knows a lot about skin care, I go to her and don't even Google my questions.

It is only when I have those trusted relationships that I can make decisions and move forward. Why does this help me? Because I have seen, tested, and established that these people are *trustworthy*. They are knowledgeable, able, and consistent. I am no longer searching through the countless gurus in search of the perfect recipe (as if my limited knowledge could assess what a good recipe is). I have trustworthy sources of information based upon the character of the expert.

Proverbs 3:5 would make no sense if it just said, "Trust with all your heart and lean not on your own understanding." The essential and core part of that verse is *trusting in the Lord* with all your heart. We are not called to live a life of faith in just anything. We are not called to put our trust in an outcome, feeling, or answer. We are called to wholly lean upon *the Lord*. We are called to trust in *the Lord*, a very specific person revealed to us through grace. Perhaps our trust in the Lord is weak because our knowledge of the Lord is small.

When we stop at "trust God" and don't take time to examine and be encouraged by the character of God, we are dropping our lives into the unknown. God never intended our faith to be blind or else He wouldn't have shown us who He is.

Maybe, though, you have false assumptions of God's character. Maybe you fear delving into who God is because you are afraid that you will be disappointed. Perhaps He is a God who teases you with good things only to take them away. Perhaps He is cold. Perhaps He is too big to care about you. Perhaps He is harsh with your silly dreams. Perhaps He is disappointed with your lack of faith.

I have struggled with thinking that God is calculating. I thought (and still think) that maybe, because I can handle it, God will give me heavy struggles. (As we all know, He gives His hardest battles to His best soldiers.) I won't turn away from Him, so He'll give me the sucky life that I fear. He wants to teach me a lesson or work through me to help someone else, so He's going to test me, abuse me, and use me. It's sometimes made me regret my maturity and wish for a silly life.

First of all, I'm thinking very highly of myself right there, thinking that I could handle these struggles better than others. Second, I am so far off from the reality of God's tender care and abundant grace. He isn't playing a game with my heart, nor is He coldly moving around puppets for His game. It was when my knowledge of His character deepened that these fears lessened.

I just had to know Him a little better.

However, we don't just know God on an intellectual level. We also get to know God emotionally. We get to *experience* who He is.

I grew up in the church and, thanks to my Mom, was so knowledgeable about the Bible that Sunday School teachers never called on me. They knew I knew. I raised one hand, squirming in my seat like Hermione Granger. When they denied me a chance to answer, I would raise the other hand with equal enthusiasm. It frustrated me that it didn't seem to matter that I knew all of the right answers.

One day, as I passed through the doors of my fifth grade Sunday School room, I questioned the point of knowing these things. There had to be more than knowing all about the Bible and God. The knowledge that I had didn't seem to get me anywhere, not fame in the classroom nor intimacy with God.

A year later, I went to a Student Life camp in Daytona Beach, Florida. It was my first youth camp, and it changed my life forever. Louie Giglio spoke on encountering God throughout the week, and I encountered God in a more powerful and intimate way than I've ever experienced Him before or since.

My church group was always late that year, and one of the last nights we were seated in the very back corner of the venue, Section 208. That night of all nights, Louie trekked up to Section 208 to finish his sermon, showing that encountering God is accessible to all in the room. The worship that night was so sweet that I thought my cheeks would fall off from smiling so much.

That week, perhaps for the first time, I not only knew God—I experienced Him. Some called it a mountaintop experience, but I never came back down from that mountain, and I have no plans to do so in the future. There, in Section 208, I saw *God.* I knew in my heart that He loved me, wouldn't give up on me, and had something good in store.

My prayer for this chapter is that you may not only deepen your understanding of God's character but that you may *experience* it for yourself. My experience in Section 208 shows that no one is too far, too late, or too small to encounter the glory of God right where they are.

Today, I want to dwell on His faithfulness, power, goodness, and consistency and how all these traits aid us to trust Him. These aren't qualities to memorize or study; they are characteristics to know, praise, and experience our God.

THE LORD IS UN-FORSAKING

"The world is starving for a yearning love, a love that remembers instead of forgets. A love that isn't tied to our loveliness. A love that gets deep underneath our messiness. A love that is bigger than the enveloping darkness we might be walking through even today. A love of which even the very best human romance is the faintest of whispers."[8]

The weeks leading up to the breakup I kept seeing the words "not forsaken." They were all over the Scripture I read, and they filled my prayers. I thought it strange that I kept thinking of these things, because as far as I could see, everything was going fine. My life seemed secure and great.

I see that now as the Lord preparing my heart not to doubt His faithfulness, even when others leave me. The un-forsaking nature of the Lord was what I clung to in

8   Dane Ortland, *Gentle and Lowly* (Wheaton, IL: Crossway, 2020), 168.

the weeks following the breakup. He built a foundation and then enabled me to stand on it.

So often, when we struggle to trust the Lord in the face of disappointment, disaster, or distress, we are struggling deep down because we think that the Lord can't possibly be *here*. Surely He turned away and forgot us for a moment. Surely He doesn't want what is best for us, because look around. How could He be here?

He has forsaken us.

And before we address the sovereignty of the Lord and His good and glorious plan, I want to sit here with you. I want to impress upon your aching heart that He has *not* forsaken you. He has not left you. He has not turned His eyes from your life, but rather has drawn nearer. Before we know why these things have happened, we get to be assured that there is no darkness too dark for Him, no confusion too much for Him, no evil too strong for Him, and no sickness too powerful for Him.

Where shall I go from your Spirit? Or where shall I flee from your presence? If I ascend to the heavens, you are there! If I make my bed in Sheol, you are there! If I take the wings of the morning and dwell in the uttermost parts of the sea, even there your hand shall lead me, and your right hand shall hold me. If I say, 'surely the darkness will cover me and the light about me be night,' even the darkness is not dark to you' the night is bright as the day, for darkness is as light with you.

—Psalm 139:7-12

Simply put, His faithfulness will always outrun your fears, failures, and faithlessness.

Perhaps, though, you do not fear that God has forsaken you because of your circumstances but because of your own inadequacies and sin. Perhaps you would have forsaken yourself long ago if you were God. Perhaps you fear that He won't want to stick around.

However, He knows that we are indeed unworthy and not enough, but He never forsakes. This is not because of what we can do for Him or how lovely we are, but because *that is who He is.* He is not disillusioned by the state of our hearts. He knows far more than we know about how needy our hearts are, how unlovely. Yet, He draws near.

Nevertheless, in your great mercies you did not make an end of them or forsake them, for you are a gracious and merciful God.

—Nehemiah 9:31

When Nehemiah is recounting the history of Israel as they ready their hearts to follow Him again, he mentions three times that the Lord did not forsake them (Neh. 9:17, 19, 31). In each of those instances the reason that Nehemiah gives isn't because that was God's plan. It isn't because He needed Israel to give Him glory. It certainly isn't because Israel was worthy then, but it also wasn't because Israel would *be* worthy.

God doesn't forsake them because He is a *gracious and merciful God*. That is simply who He is. He bases His promises not on our actions but on His character. It is the guarantee. He is a God who doesn't forsake. He is a God who deals mercifully with His people. He is a God who saw the depth of our sin and instead of turning away came close. He touched the lepers, saw the desolate, and didn't turn from the foreigner.

Our confidence and hope are not that we are going to be unforsaken in life by others, our jobs, our bodies, or our dreams. Our confidence and hope aren't even that God won't forsake us as long as it is advantageous to Him. Our confidence and hope are that God will never forsake us because *that is who He is*.

This is an important shift in our understanding because sometimes we, be it knowingly or unknowingly, think that our very act of trusting the Lord makes us more worthy of His good favor. We think that our response to the gospel makes us more worthy recipients.

It's not about us; it's about God. He is a God who sticks close. He is a God who doesn't give up on us. He is a God who gives us confidence to draw near. He is a God who loves us to the end. He is a God who delights in us. He is a God of unshakable, unbreakable covenant. He is a God who doesn't waver in His decisions. This is who He is.

> You shall be a crown of beauty in the hand of the LORD and a royal diadem in the hand of your God. You shall no more be termed Forsaken and your land shall no more be termed Desolate, but you shall be called My Delight is in Her and your land Married, for the LORD delights in you, and your land shall be married; For as a young man marries a young woman, so shall your sons marry you, and as the bridegroom rejoices over the bride, so shall your God rejoice over you.
>
> —ISAIAH 62:3-5

He will not forsake us, not because of who we are, what He gains, or what makes sense, but because *that is who He is*. We can rest, live, mourn, and grow in this truth.

THE LORD IS ALL-KNOWING AND
ALL-POWERFUL

I'm not here to crack the puzzle on the sovereignty of God, but I question if it's truly a puzzle after all. Maybe it is a tapestry that we only see a small piece of from behind. Jerry Bridges uses a neat illustration to describe how we only have a small timeframe in which we incompletely view the world, whereas God is outside of time and sees all things.

"The underside of a weaving usually makes no sense. Even the upper side makes little sense if we view just a tiny piece. Only God sees the upper side, and only He sees the entire fabric with its complete pattern. Therefore, we must learn to trust Him to work out all the details of history to His glory, knowing that His glory and our good are bound up together."[9]

God knows. He knows. And knowledge is a pretty trustworthy thing. That's why we (at least should) trust our teachers, because they *know* more than us. However, our teachers don't know *everything*, thus we don't completely trust them. God, however, made the universe and is knowledgeable, aware, and in control of *all things*. He isn't Doctor Strange; it doesn't take Him 10,000 calculations to figure out the best outcome. His character

---

9 Jerry Bridges, *Trusting God* (Colorado Springs, CO: NavPress, 2016), 81–82.

is one that is outside of time. He knows the past, the present, and the future as if it has already happened.

That's almost scary trustworthy.

Let's return to Psalm 139: "O LORD, you have searched me and known me! *You know* when I sit down and when I rise up; *you discern* my thoughts from afar. You search out my path and my lying down and are acquainted with *all* my ways. Even before a word is on my tongue, behold, O LORD, *you know it altogether.* You hem me in, behind and before, and lay your hand upon me. Such *knowledge* is too wonderful for me; it is high; I cannot attain it" (Ps. 139:1–6, emphasis mine).

The Lord is thoroughly, intimately, sovereignly knowledgeable about our lives, futures, hearts, and pasts. He knows when we take the long way home to cry a bit in the car. He also knows when we really wanted to flip off that driver in front of us. He knows our thoughts, ways, and dreams. He knows what we are going to do before we do it.

He also knows how our lives interact with the lives of others. He knew that today I would be walking on the treadmill at the very moment one of my friends walked up needing to talk. He knew that my parents would meet at Baylor University and my mom would give my crazy dad a chance. He knew that a slow and painful season would lead to me typing up this very book.

He also knows what's coming. He knows if there's a hurricane in the Gulf right now (I dearly hope not). He knows the days marked out for us, both the wonderful ones and the hard ones.

David ends this section of Psalm 139 with "such knowledge is too wonderful for me." The knowledge of the Lord is too big for us to grasp. His ways are higher than our ways, His thoughts higher than our thoughts. We see a small part of the underside of the tapestry of life, but the Lord sees the whole picture. We struggle to comprehend His plan within our minds because we are stuck in time, and He works outside of time.

This distinction has brought me much peace with the sovereignty of God. I do believe Him to be absolutely sovereign. But the problem with our understanding of things like "predestination" is found in the word itself. "Pre" is a timeline kind of word. There's a before, a during, and an after. But God, being outside of time, isn't limited to the timeline. Thus, our understanding of things like predestination and sovereignty is limited because we think within time about something that is simply too big for our little heads.

Rather than get discouraged about the magnitude of God's knowledge, it should encourage us to trust Him because He knows the way. If we think of our lives as a journey, do we trust a navigator who doesn't know the way? No. Thus we prove ourselves, our friends, our contemporaries, and philosophers limited because absolutely no one in this world can predict the future.

Only God knows the way. However, we can know God.

More than just being all-knowing, the Lord is able to act perfectly in accordance with His knowledge. As it says in Isaiah 14:27, "For the LORD of hosts has purposed, and who will annul it? His hand is stretched out, and who will turn it back?" And in 1 Thessalonians 5:24, it says, "He who calls you is faithful and he will surely do it."

The Lord is all-powerful to change hearts (Exod. 3:21-22, 12:35-36; Ezra 1:1). God is all-powerful to control weather, sickness, and disasters (Jer. 14:22; Job 38-41; Ps. 147). God is all-powerful in politics and the nations (2 Chron. 20:6; Acts 4:27-28; Rom. 13:1; Dan. 4:17). Thus, He is all-powerful to bless your career. He is all-powerful to bless your struggle. He is all-powerful to bless you with children. He is all-powerful to bless you in infertility. He is all-powerful to bring marriage into your life. He is all-powerful to use singleness in your life.

The Lord is the perfect Navigator of our lives. He is able to light the way because He knows the way. He is able to keep our feet from slipping on the way because of His strong hand.

THE LORD IS GOOD

Knowing that God is powerful only establishes trust in Him if we also know that He is *good*. After all, He could be perfectly capable of all things but choose not to do what is good for us. He could be perfectly knowledgeable of all things but not have our best intentions at heart.

This is particularly hard to see when life is hard. How could an all-knowing, all-powerful God let _____ happen? Surely that means that He isn't good.

Again, I ask us to take a step back and remember that God *is* good. It's not just that God does good things and not just that we will see everything He does as good in the moment. No, we must first come to the truth that God *is* good. Thus, the gifts He gives are good. Thus, the plans He makes are good. Let's take it one step further and sit in the truth that God desires *our* good. That is also who He is. Thus, the gifts He gives to *us* are good. Thus, the plans he makes for *us* are good.

This poem by Florence May Gibbs and popularized by Corrie Ten Boom illustrates the matter:

My life is but a weaving
between my Lord and me;
I cannot choose the colors
He worketh steadily.

Oft times He weaveth sorrow
And I, in foolish pride,
Forget He sees the upper,
And I the under side.

Not 'til the loom is silent
And the shuttles cease to fly,
Shall God unroll the canvas
And explain the reason why.

The dark threads are as needful
In the Weaver's skillful hand,
As the threads of gold and silver
In the pattern He has planned.

He knows, He loves, He cares,
Nothing this truth can dim.
He gives His very best to those
Who leave the choice with Him.[10]

Joseph, at the end of his life, reflected upon how his brothers sold him into slavery where he was treated

---

10 Florence May Gibbs, "Weaving," Discover Poetry, last
    modified January 1, 2023.
    https://discoverpoetry.com/poems/florence-may-alt/weaving/.

poorly, forgotten about, and manipulated. He looked at what God was doing and deemed it *good*.

> As for you [his brothers], you meant evil against me, but God meant it for good, to bring it about that many people should be kept alive as they are today.
>
> —GENESIS 50:20

This demonstrates that God's goodness isn't limited to perfect situations. It penetrates the disappointments and directs them for good. It saturates the disasters and turns them to His goodness. It speaks through distress to a greater picture, one of goodness and mercy.

> Oh, taste and see that the Lord is good! Blessed is the man who takes refuge in him!
>
> —PSALM 34:8

If we ever forget the goodness of the Lord, we need only look to the Cross.

For whatever way you think that God is holding out on you, in whatever small crevice of your heart that you believe the lie that God withholds good from your life, let's learn to speak the *truth*.

God is *not* withholding goodness for you.

How do I know that?

The Cross says so.

For He held nothing back on the Cross as He died for the consequences for our sins. He held nothing back as He hung, suffered, and died. Toward the humiliating spectacle of the Cross we orient our souls when we're tempted to think that God is holding back from us anything perfect, pleasing, and acceptable.

> He who would not spare his own son, but gave him up for us all, how will he not also with him graciously give us all things?
>
> —ROMANS 8:32

Dwell here a moment. For the *joy* set before him, Christ endured the Cross, scorning its shame (Heb. 12:2). We can't grasp how dark that moment was, how heavy the sin was, or how deep His love is. If He was going to hold back, that was the moment. But Christ held nothing back as He bled for our sins. God held nothing back as He gave His only Son for our redemption.

There on the Cross, we see on full display the goodness of God and His dedication for our souls to have what is best. There we see on full display that God is not holding out on us, but that He desires good for our lives. *He* is what is good for our lives. If He didn't hold back then, we can be confident that He isn't holding back now. If the Cross didn't scare off His commitment to our hearts, then something like sickness, singleness, or layoffs won't scare Him either.

He isn't teasing us by withholding things like love, health, security, and clarity for a time (or forever). He isn't playing a game with our hearts. He knows our hearts. He knows how hard the waiting is. He knows how the unanswered questions are hard. He knows how the pain of the unexpected toils of life is hard.

But in a glorious way, He uses the hard for good. What man intends for evil He uses for glory. Thus, because of the imperishable, undefiled, and unfading promise of the gospel, we are called to a sure and living hope in times of suffering (1 Pet. 1).

Tell our doubts of God's goodness to shatter at the feet of the Cross, because there we can *know* that God's plan is for His glory and our good. There we can know that God is not holding back His love for us, but that even suffering and dark places (for what was darker than the Cross?) are gloriously essential to His plan.

THE LORD IS UNCHANGING

Imagine you are strapped to a harness and standing on the edge of a mountain cliff. Beneath you lies a mountain with all of its ridges and beauty. There's a small river running through the valley, but it's far off and down below. Above you is a cable that your harness attaches to. You are about to go ziplining through the mountains.

There's a lot of trust when ziplining. You trust that the cable is strong enough to hold you. You trust that the harness won't break. You trust that the crew won't decide to cut the cable when you're out there. Now, you've seen a dozen people go down the zipline without a problem, so realistically you *know* that the cable is strong enough, the harness won't break, and the crew doesn't have a death wish for you.

But you still have to trust a bit as you take that jump off the mountain.

What are you trusting?

You are trusting that these things *haven't changed*. You are trusting that, just as you've seen before, the cable, harness, and crew are the same. You're trusting that they are unchanging.

In the same way, trusting God is only as good as He is unchanging. For if the character of God could change, then the very core of our trust could crumble. After all, we know and trust Him as a loving God today, but if there was a possibility of Him changing tomorrow, then our trust is shallow at best and fearful at worst.

We have confidence that God never changes. He doesn't trick us like shifting shadows (James 1:17). He doesn't change His mind (Num. 23:19). His Word echoes true for all eternity. His character remains the same yesterday, today, and tomorrow.

We don't know what that's like because all we know are people who change. We are always growing or declining. People around us appear one way and change the next day. We are unsure of who we are right now, let alone who we will be forever, but God never changes. He's always been and always will be the *exact same*. Circumstances don't change him. He doesn't evolve or grow, for that would be to suggest that there was a time he was *less-than*. He doesn't have to learn through trial-and-error, for there is no learning and certainly no error with the Lord.

The verse I've clung to dearly when life changes dramatically is Hebrews 13:8: "Jesus Christ is the same yesterday, today, and tomorrow." It was the only verse I could repeat to myself the night my boyfriend broke up with me. That verse echoed in my brain in the wake of change. This verse is a rock to stand upon when the world turns upside down. This is a truth to build upon when storms knock down your dreams. This is a God to trust when life and people change and let you down.

I was talking to a friend today about how she trusts the Lord.

"I remember that He has provided thus far," she said, "And that He will do that again and again." She could trust God because she knew that He would be the same yesterday, today, and forever. She recounted all of the ways He was faithful, sovereign, and good before in her life and knew that the same was true today. Only in our unchanging God can we rest assured that He will forever be un-forsaking, all-knowing, and good. If He could change, then our confidence would be for nothing.

The Bible is full of remembering the Lord's unchanging nature and recounting His works. Nehemiah 9, as mentioned earlier in this chapter, is a beautiful example of God's people recounting His works. Stephen's speech in Acts 7 recounts the unchanging character of the Lord through history, leading up to the pinnacle of Christ. Consider with me that even the genealogies we tend to skip are founded in the Lord's unchanging character. Generation to generation passed, and His purposes stood firm. Through each new line of family, through each inconsistent human era, God remained the same. His character and heart were unchanging. He did not become calloused because of our rebellion nor lax in our disobedience. He is independent of time and circumstances.

Psalm 136 is a concise and powerful reminder of the unchanging nature of God throughout time. It starts with "Give thanks to the Lord, for he is good, for his steadfast love endures forever." From there, the Psalmist details how God's steadfast love was the same in Creation, the Exodus, and the creation of Israel.

> To him who by understanding made the heavens, for his steadfast love endures forever; . . . To him who struck down the firstborn of Egypt, for his steadfast love endures forever; . . . to him who struck down great kings, for his love endures forever; . . . it is he who remembered us in our low estate, for his steadfast love endures forever.
>
> —PSALM 136:5, 10, 17, 23

The foundation of this praise is the steadfast love of the Lord, which endures forever. That is why He created the world. That is why He rescued Israel. That is why He paves the way. And that is why the Psalmist can trust the Lord to continue to rescue.

In Hebrews 6, we are reminded that the promises of God are doubly trustworthy because God's character and purposes are *unchanging,* and He has backed up His oath with *Himself.* Since He doesn't change, His promises won't change. Since He cannot lie, His oath stands firm.

So when God desired to show more convincingly to the heirs of the promise the unchangeable character of his purpose, he guaranteed it with an oath, so that by two unchangeable things, in which it is impossible for God to lie, we who have fled for refuge might have strong encouragement to hold fast to the hope set before us. We have this as a sure and steadfast anchor of the soul.

—Hebrews 6:17–19

The world may change, we may change, others around us may change, but He's not changing. He's a sure foundation and steady rock. He's not going to change His mind about His faithfulness. He's not going to be less sovereign tomorrow. He's not going to retract His goodness next week. My friends, the Lord is the same yesterday, today, and tomorrow. His character is unflinchingly and unswervingly faithful, powerful, knowing, and good. Rest in that. Trust in that. Live in that.

There is so much I wish to say about the gloriously beautiful nature of God's character, but these four characteristics have impacted me the most when I struggle to trust God. I pray that this makes us all hungry for more of who God is, that we may be filled with all spiritual wisdom and understanding (Col. 1:9). A.W. Tozer's book *The Knowledge of the Holy* is a good resource for those wishing to fix their minds on the character of God. The first sentence of that book says, "What comes to our minds when we think about God is the most important thing about us."[11]

How true is that?

GROWING ROOTS

▶ What characteristic of God touched your heart in this chapter?

▶ What attribute of God is hardest for you to believe?

▶ How can you put practices in your life to help you know the Lord better?

---

11 A.W. Tozer, *The Knowledge of the Holy* (San Francisco, CA: HarperOne, 1978), 13.

CHAPTER FOUR

Trusting 100 Percent

Will You Walk on the Water?

All my chips and chipped pieces
On the table
All my trust and trusted vices
On the table
All my heart and heartbreak
On the table
I can put it all on the table because
You first put it all
On the Cross

I went to a wedding not too long after a breakup, knowing it would be hard. I knew that I would be tempted to compare my life with the happy lives of the couple. I knew that I would be tempted to doubt the goodness of God to me. I knew that I would be tempted to flirt with all the single guys. I knew I would be tempted to distrust the Lord's will for me regarding marriage. With that in mind, I didn't want to go. But I went anyway.

I prayed before attending the wedding—over the couple, over my single friends, and lastly over my own heart. In this time of prayer, a question lingered over my mind. It led me to trust, it exposed my own distrust, and it gave me gutsy faith to celebrate something I longed for with others.

Do I trust the Lord 100 percent?

I sat there, in my doubts of God's goodness, worries about the future, and desires to grow in grace. I felt as if I was on a precipice. To hold back felt surer. To fall forward felt like accepting hardship. I stilled my heart, whispered to my soul, "100 percent," and took the step.

I went to that wedding not with a date but with my parents. As all of my friends arrived with their dates and husbands, I whispered to my soul, "100 percent." As the bride walked down the aisle to one of my favorite love songs, I whispered to my soul, "100 percent." As they exchanged precious vows, I whispered to my soul, "100 percent." As I could so clearly envision myself standing up there, I whispered to my soul, "100 percent." There was something about this full commitment that gave my heart courage.

A girl attending the wedding came up to me that night. She had also recently gone through a breakup. I could see the pain in her eyes as she wrestled with the "why not me" mindset.

"100 percent," I whispered to her. "We can trust Him 100 percent."

A few days later, as I was contemplating this commitment, I got into my car. I am a huge Spotify girl, and I never listen to the radio. However, the radio turned on for a few seconds that day before I had time to connect my phone, and the voice of the host on K-Love asked, "What if you trusted God 100 percent?"

Needless to say, I listened to K-Love that day.

This leads me to ask you the same question. Do you trust the Lord 100 percent? What would that look like in your life? I ask it this way, because it makes us examine our hearts, it requires us to be honest, and it challenges us towards gutsy faith. It's extreme, yes, but remember how we defined trust?

> Trust in the Lord with *all* your heart and lean not on your own understanding.
>
> —PROVERBS 3:5

All your heart.

The Lord doesn't desire our hearts in part, but in full. He doesn't desire part of our trust, but all of it. He doesn't desire us to halfway enjoy the blessings of His peace—He wants us to overflow with spiritual blessings (Eph. 1:3). He is jealous for our hearts, as it says in James 4:5: "Or do you suppose it is to no purpose that the Scripture says, 'he yearns jealously over the spirit that he has made to dwell in us?'"

Yes, 100 percent is extreme, but the Lord extremely wants us to trust in Him.

This gutsy faith reminds me of Peter. Jesus had just fed the 5,000 when He sends the disciples ahead of Him on the water. A storm emerges, tossing their boat to and fro late into the night. That's when Jesus shows up. His mode of transportation in the middle of a storm on the water? Walking.

The disciples are fearful when they see a figure on the water. Jesus cries out, "Take heart; it is I. Do not be afraid."

"And Peter answered him, 'Lord, if it is you, command me to come to you on the water.' He said, 'Come.' So Peter got out of the boat and walked on the water and came to Jesus. But when he saw the wind, he was afraid, and beginning to sink he cried out, 'Lord, save me.' Jesus immediately reached out his hand and took hold of him, saying to him, 'O you of little faith, why did you doubt?' And when they got into the boat, the wind ceased. And those in the boat worshiped him, saying, 'Truly you are the Son of God' (Matt. 14:28-33).

I love Peter. He's boisterous and impulsive and committed. I consider us to be similar in many ways. When Peter sees the Lord and the invitation to be all in, Peter takes it. He steps out of the boat. He's seen nothing but choppy, rough waters all night, but as soon as he sees Christ, the storm seems insignificant. That's some gutsy faith right there.

As I invite you to trust the Lord 100 percent, let's examine three truths as revealed in Peter's story to help us reframe the narrative in our minds and step out onto the water. Let's learn to choose to trust God all the way.

HE IS 100 PERCENT WORTHY OF OUR TRUST

Is this the first time Peter experienced Jesus on a boat? Nope. A few chapters before the walking-on-water fiasco, Peter experienced Jesus in a similar fashion. See Matthew 8:23-27:

And when he [Jesus] got into the boat, his disciples followed him. And behold, there arose a great storm on the sea, so that the boat was being swamped by the waves; but he was asleep. And they went and woke him, saying, "Save us, Lord; we are perishing." And he said to them, "Why are you afraid? O you of little faith." Then he rose and rebuked the winds and the sea, and there was a great calm. And the men marveled, saying, "What sort of man is this, that even the winds and the sea obey him?"

Before Peter asked to walk on the water, he experienced Jesus's power over the wind and the waves. He saw that Jesus was trustworthy and powerful. These passages build off each other. Both involve a storm at sea. Both involve Jesus's rebuke of faith. Both end with the disciples marveling at Jesus. I do not think we are supposed to take Peter walking on the water without also remembering that he already *knew* Jesus could calm the waves.

Trusting the Lord 100 percent can sound foolish. It can sound, at first glance, like blind faith. But, as discussed before, *God shows us how trustworthy He is.* He shows us through His Word, He shows us through the church, and He shows us through His faithful love to us in our past experiences.

When I challenge us to trust the Lord 100 percent, it isn't a call to abandon logic or to throw ourselves into the unknown. I challenge us with this because I am assured that the Lord is 100 percent trustworthy.

Peter had seen enough of Christ to know that He was trustworthy. He had seen Christ's miracles, heard his teaching, witnessed His authority, and been in His presence long enough to know that Christ was Lord, powerful, and caring. The taste of the miraculously multiplied bread was still on his lips when Peter ventured out onto the waters. Peter didn't step out into the water for just anybody. He stepped out onto the water because *Christ* was beckoning him.

Here's the crazy part: Peter *did walk on water.* With Christ as his focus, he did what is humanly, what is anatomically, impossible to do. The other disciples stayed in the boat, but Peter came out. The rest of the story can give Peter a bad rep, but let us not forget to be amazed at his step of obedience.

IT IS 100 PERCENT UNFULFILLING TO TRUST IN ANYTHING ELSE

These aren't the only two experiences with Peter and Jesus and a boat. In fact, Peter's first recorded experience with Jesus in Matthew takes place at sea. Matthew 4:18-20 says: "While walking by the Sea of Galilee, he saw two brothers, Simon (who is called Peter) and Andrew, his brother, casting a net into the sea, for they were fishermen. And he said to them, 'Follow me, and I will make you fishers of men.' Immediately they left their nets and followed him."

Right here, Peter makes a choice: he decides that Jesus is better. Jesus is better than his old life. Jesus is better than Peter's illusion of control. Jesus is better than staying in the boat. More than that, Peter also declares the opposite: it is *not worth it* to trust in himself, the boat, or the familiar ways.

Not only must we realize that the Lord is trustworthy, but we must also realize that all else is *untrustworthy*. Our abilities can be untrustworthy. Others can be untrustworthy. Outcomes, feelings, and answers can be untrustworthy.

The most helpful thing I find about asking if I trust in the Lord 100 percent is that it helps me figure out where else I'm putting my trust. If we truly trust the Lord, we won't be worried about these other things. Therefore, when we worry, there is an element of distrust in God and misplaced trust in something else. If I think I only trust the Lord 40 percent with my career, where is the other 60 percent going? Is it going to my strengths? Because my strengths will fail.

Even youths shall faint and be weary, and young men shall fall exhausted; but they who wait for the LORD shall renew their strength; they shall mount up with wings like eagles; they shall run and not be weary; they shall walk and not faint.

—ISAIAH 40:30-31

Put not your trust in princess, in a son of man, in whom there is no salvation.

—PSALM 146:3

Is my trust in circumstances? That it'll all just work out?

Woe to those who go down to Egypt for help, and rely on horses, who trust in chariots because they are many and in horsemen because they are very strong, but they do not look to the Holy One of Israel, or consult the LORD!

—ISAIAH 31:1

Is my trust in the government?

Behold, you rely on the staff of this crushed reed, even on Egypt, on which if a man leans, it will go into his hand and pierce it. So is Pharaoh king of Egypt to all who rely on him.

—ISAIAH 36:6

Look long enough at the world, and it morphs into a shifting shadow. But look long enough at the Lord, and you morph to become Christlike—and Christ doesn't change like the shifting shadows (James 1:17). We need to be clear with ourselves where else we are putting our trust so that we may see its fruitlessness and reorient ourselves around Christ.

Hold no illusions about the world. It cannot save you from the water. Your 401K can't save you. Your secure marriage can't save you. Your 4.0 GPA can't save you. Your adoring dog can't save you. The world, indeed your own heart, will try to tell you that these things are trustworthy, but we are called not to live like the world but to follow Christ.

If we believe Christ to be completely trustworthy, it would actually be foolish of us to put our trust in anything else. If God is *best,* why would we choose to want anything less? If God has what is best for me, then why would I worry about when I get married? If He is trustworthy for you, and you really believe that, why would you trust in something else?

As soon as Peter looked away from Christ, his ability to trust was weakened. Suddenly he knew that he was in over his head. He couldn't swim in water like this. Thus, he started to sink. He sank because he began to put his trust and his sight on his own abilities rather than on Christ.

How often do we do this? Far more often than I would like to admit. One moment, full of gutsy faith, we take that step out. We train our minds to trust the Lord 100 percent. The next moment, though, we second-guess those risks and tremble in fear.

One minute, I could rejoice in another's marriage, and the next, I was crying about the absence of it in my life. One day I'm sacrificing my time with joy and the next, I'm worried about how to get it all done. One month I'm letting God define what is good, and the next month, I start to define it.

Does Christ leave Peter to drown in his unbelief? Not at all! Christ pulls him back up with a reprimand, an encouragement, and a miracle. First, He calls Peter out on his faith. This wasn't an issue of the water being too rough, it was an issue of Peter's faith wavering. Then, He encourages Peter to trust. *Why did you doubt?* He says. *I had you.* Christ points to His ability, not Peter's, as the encouragement to keep going. Then, He calms the storm. He shows Himself undeniably greater than the choppy waters and worries of life. He shows Himself to be absolutely trustworthy in the storm. He is Lord over the storm when it's raging on, and He is Lord over the storm when the seas are quiet.

Living in trust isn't a one-and-done decision. It is constantly putting before our eyes the character of Christ and of the Father, recognizing that everything else is untrustworthy. It is step-by-step faith, moment-by-moment trust. We get to train our minds to turn to Christ when less-than-trustworthy things vie for our attention.

IT IS 100 PERCENT GOOD FOR US TO TRUST HIM

The walking on the water scene also isn't the last scene we see Jesus and Peter on a boat. John 21 details the last recorded time Peter and Jesus shared a beachside moment together on Earth:

Just as day was breaking, Jesus stood on the shore; yet the disciples did not know that it was Jesus. Jesus said to them, "Children, do you have any fish?" They answered him, "No." He said to them, "Cast the net on the right side of the boat, and you will find some." So they cast it, and now they were not able to haul it in, because of the quantity of fish. The disciple whom Jesus loved therefore said to Peter, "It is the Lord!" When Simon Peter heard that it was the Lord, he put on his outer garment, for he was stripped for work, and threw himself into the sea.

—JOHN 21:4–8

Peter does love jumping out of boats, doesn't he?

At the end of the gospels, Peter's change is stark. He is still all-in, but this time he goes all the way. He reaches the shore and meets the hard truth that the storms coming up in his life will be hard. However, his resurrected Savior is before him. Christ is alive! Thus, Peter counts the cost as *worth it.*

Perhaps in our struggle to trust God, we think that it's not worth it. We stay on the sidelines and wait for a time when it's easier and more urgent. We don't take risks in our faith because that's just easier for other people to do. We'll watch them. We play it safe. We wait for when it feels "right."

God didn't create us to default to fear and risk avoidance. Piper says in *Don't Waste Your Life,* "It is the will of God that we be uncertain about how life on earth will turn out for us. And therefore, it is the will of the Lord that we take risks for the cause of God."[12] Trusting Him 100 percent isn't a bad deal for us; it is His will for

---

12 John Piper, *Don't Waste Your Life,* (Wheaton, IL: Crossway Books, 2018), 80.

us. Jumping into His plans won't leave us in want or wishing we had stayed in the boat.

Trusting Him 100 percent is 100 percent *good for us.*

It was an ordeal for Peter to walk on the waves during the storm. Peter could have reasoned that Jesus was coming to the boat anyway. Why go out to meet him? It is because Peter counted Christ as worth the risk that Peter stepped out on the water. The other disciples didn't share Peter's impulsive behaviors but notice the ending of this passage: "And those in the boat worshiped him, saying, 'Truly you are the Son of God'" (Matt. 14:33).

It was good that Peter took that risk. Even though he did it imperfectly, Christ still got the glory. As the disciples continued in their journeys with Christ and the early church, I wonder how often they, especially Peter, thought back on that moment. When they faced persecution, did they remember how Christ calmed the storm? When Peter denied Christ, did he remember how Christ's arm pulled him back up even in his doubts? When Peter stood in front of the crowd at Pentecost, did he remember how Jesus was worth the waves?

The risk to trust was worth it all, both for Peter and for those watching.

Your risk to trust is worth it, both for your life and for those watching your life.

There is so much good waiting on the other side of trusting the Lord.

* * *

So, do you trust the Lord 100 percent?

More than just identifying ways we distrust and reminding us of the truth, this question paves new pathways in our minds. When we determine to trust the Lord 100 percent, we're pre-deciding to operate in the truth of who God is. We've already made up our minds that when we're tempted to compare our broken love story to our friend's happily ever after, we will redirect our thoughts to the goodness of Christ, as displayed on the cross. We've already chosen to think about the faithfulness of the Lord when we're anxious about what turn our careers will take. We get to pre-decide to redirect our thoughts to trust the Lord when questions about our health, family, or disasters come up.

My dad is the biggest voice of "pre-decision" for me. We both struggle with trying to make perfect choices and then second-guessing them. However, sometimes we have to pre-decide something and then follow through even when we don't feel like it. I can pre-decide to write every night even when I don't feel like it. We can pre-decide to leave at nine even if we don't feel like it. We can pre-decide not to listen to sad songs that make us feel in the dumps. That's the power of pre-decision; it alleviates the mental struggle and simplifies the decision-making process.

Scripture is clear that following Christ means taking every thought captive (2 Cor. 10:5), setting our minds on things above (Col. 3:2), and training ourselves to, instead of worrying, dwell upon the truth (Phil. 4:6-8). We will talk about this more in-depth later, but we get to remind ourselves that we are all in. **We get to take Him at His Word.** We get to jump into the water of God's care for us, confident in His faithful, powerful, good, and unchanging arms. We get to walk upon the waves, sure of one thing: Christ. The rest will come.

When we jump into the arms of our Father, we are declaring to ourselves and to the world that we don't just know intellectually that God is trustworthy, we are getting out of the boat. Step by step, we decide to trust the Lord. Moment by moment, we declare that Christ is indeed Lord and more worthy of our attention than any storm.

GROWING ROOTS

► What percent would you say you trust the Lord with your life? Your relationships? Your job? Your family?

► What are the things and who are the people you trust instead of God?

► How would pre-deciding to trust God change your week?

CHAPTER FIVE

Drawing Near with Small Faith

Come to Him with Whatever Percentage of Trust You Have

Crying at church is a strange phenomenon.
One may think you particularly religious,
but sometimes you are simply needy.
One may think that you are especially repentant,
but sometimes you are only tired.

I cried at church today,
not necessarily out conviction or sorrow
but out of need.
Weariness tainted my worship,
but I cried and came nonetheless,
and God met me there.

Sometimes I think that I can impress God. My tendency is to want to impress. I want to impress my dad by how I work. I want to impress the church by how I serve. I want to impress the world by how I post. So, subtly, I think that I can impress God, too. Sure, there's hardship, but I have faith. Sure, I'm overwhelmed, but I can go to Scripture. Sure, I'm disappointed and discouraged, but God doesn't need that. He needs my praise, faith, and work. I don't have time to be despondent.

I pulled up in my driveway at 11:30 p.m. after what should have been a great day, but which was, in reality, hard. It was my sister's birthday, and we had a great day of celebrating, but there was this sulking heaviness that I couldn't shake. The pressures of life were making me crack, and my inability was showing through. I felt the heaviness of all my friends' lives, the pressure to be there for them in the right way, and the questions about my own life that I couldn't sort out, either. I expected to be over heartbreak by then, but it lingered. I expected my business to pick up by then, but it was slow. I expected my ankle to be healed by then, but the bright blue kinesthetic tape wrapped around it said otherwise.

I got so used to carrying the weight of the world on my shoulders that I forgot that wasn't a weight I was meant to carry. I was weighed down with sadness to the point that I couldn't get out of the car, so I sat there and cried. As tears rolled down my nose and hit the steering wheel, I released my grip on my own goodness and was simply needy before the Lord. Something shifted for me that night. In that moment, I wasn't afraid of my own neediness. What the Lord taught me that night transformed my life. Here's an excerpt of my thoughts from that June night:

[I think that] the Lord deserves better than this. Where is my obedience? I should really get my act together. What am I doing with my life? Why can't I motivate myself to just do better? But it's all okay. I trust Him. I'm thankful to Him. I'm directing my heart to praise Him.

And this is good, but perhaps at times, subtly and softly, I begin to think that the Lord needs me, and I can't come to him in need until it's figured out with an inspirational Instagram message. Perhaps if I poorly receive grace it's worse than not receiving it at all.

The truth is, although I long to trust the Lord 100 percent, sometimes I only have 10 percent of trust, a mustard seed of trust, or a sliver of dependency. Although the goal is to trust the Lord with all our hearts, the reality is often far from that. The reality is that we often stay up into the night wondering if it'll all work out. We get anxious at stoplights because we already feel behind. We may trust the Lord with the decision to move, but we struggle to trust Him with that one pile of junk that we haven't organized yet. The reality is that our grades, deadlines, disappointments, and dreams seem more urgent than trusting the Lord. We're so used to holding everything tightly that we fear to open our hands. They're stiff in their clenched position.

The Lord isn't disappointed with this struggle. In fact, He draws us in right now and, from one percent to the next, increases our trust. One of the most detrimental lies in faith is the subtle lie that we need to clean ourselves up before we come to God, that we have to get things right before we can be a part of His kingdom. There is no interview process for God's family. There are simply adoption papers signed because of the Cross. That is all. We were dead in our sins and trespasses (rebellion and failures) when God, out of *His* mercy, made us alive in Him (Eph. 2:5). We did nothing to get that grace initially, and we do nothing to keep it. Again, our response to the gospel doesn't make us more worthy recipients.

Friend, with our small faith, we are instructed to draw near, know the Lord, and ask for more trust. Take that 1 percent of trust that you have and place it in open hands. Or take your pride, that *you can do it* attitude, and place it in your open hands. I venture to guess that by the end of this chapter, those who think they have little will see *all* that is theirs in Christ, and those who think they have it all together will see *all* they need in Christ.

DRAW NEAR

Many people drew near to Jesus during His ministry, but one in particular illustrates boldness in the face of weakness:

> And Jesus asked his father, "How long has this been happening to him?" And he said, "From childhood. And it has often cast him into fire and into water, to destroy him. But if you can do anything, have compassion on us and help us." And Jesus said to him, "'If you can'! All things are possible for one who believes." Immediately the father of the child cried out[a] and said, "I believe; help my unbelief!"
>
> —MARK 9:21-24

The father in this passage had tried all the things and exhausted his resources to cure the son whom he loved. He couldn't bear the thought of seeing his son harm himself again. When he heard about Jesus, he hurried over. Maybe Jesus could help him. However, he first met Jesus's disciples, for Jesus was on the mountain with Peter, James, and John. The remaining disciples could do nothing to help the boy, and the crowd started to argue.

Then Jesus came. The father straightened up his shoulders and tried again, just like he'd been trying all this time. He pushed through the crowd and approached Jesus himself.

He drew near with confidence and need, just like Hebrews 4:16 says: "Let us then with confidence draw near to the throne of grace that we may receive mercy and find grace to help in time of need."

Historically speaking, when people encounter the throne of God, they are anything but confident. They fall on their face (Ezek.1:28). They are crushed by their sinfulness and pressed with the holiness of the Lord (Isa. 6:5). It is a blaring truth that they are dirty, small, and unworthy in front of a pure, huge, perfect God.

But in Hebrews 4, the Lord instructs us to be *confident* before Him. He is like a father who wants his son to show him his batting skills, even if the father is much better. He is like a mother who loves to see her daughter's drawings, even though they are little scribbles with a neon green crayon all over the page.

What is this confidence? What is this childlike joy in our inability? One might assume that this confidence comes from the grace of God bestowed upon us through Christ, and whereas that *is* our right-standing before God, let's take a closer look at Hebrews 4:16: "Let us then with confidence draw near to the throne of grace that we may receive mercy and find grace to help in time of need."

Notice the order. We *first* draw near with confidence and *then* we receive his mercy and grace. We are called to bring our messy, selfish, unsure selves before the radiance of God. We are called to draw near to that which melts our heart and exposes our sinfulness. *Then* He pours grace upon us. Then He helps us in His mercy. But first we come. And that is terrifying.

I think it's scary to be vulnerable before the Lord because of pride and fear. Pride tells us that we should have it all together. Pride may sound like, "I've got this," but it could also sound like, "I should have this." Both the self-confident and the self-aware person look inwards when God calls us to look at the Cross.

Fear may also stop us in our tracks on our way to the Cross—fear that it's too late for us. Fear that we should know more than we do. Fear that we've done too much against the Lord for Him to be for us now. Fear that we're fake, forced, or faithless.

How, then, do we inch near to Him, all our sin, fears, and pride exposed? How do we quiet the prideful and fearful thoughts? How can we give him our little bit of trust and ask for more? How can we, like children, show

Him our little scribbles and be confident that He desires them?

Our confidence flows from *the person of Christ*.

When we were still stuck in our inability and sin, Christ *came to us*. He drew near to us. He closed the gap, tore the curtain, and touched our faraway hearts. You may feel ashamed or undone, but He feels ready to wrap you in His arms. He left heaven for you. You may feel like you've wasted too many chances, but what He has done, He has done once and for all. We have great confidence in the person of Christ to draw near to the throne.

In fact, right before Hebrews 4 says to draw near, it points to Jesus Christ, who first drew near to us, first was tempted like we are, and first was given as a replacement for our sin (Heb. 4:15). Later in Hebrews, we are called forward to run our race, fixing our eyes on *Jesus* (Heb. 12:1–2).

Let's look again to Isaiah. When Isaiah came before the throne of God, he fell on his face and said, "Woe is me, for I am a man of unclean lips and I live among a people of unclean lips" (Isa. 6:5). But he still drew near. He still listened to the Lord. More than that, he didn't hesitate to make himself a vessel of the Lord's calling.

Somehow, he found the confidence to enter into the story. Why?

John 12:41 enlightens us on this. "Isaiah said these things because he saw his glory and spoke of him [Christ]."

Isaiah saw the glory of Christ and the gospel, although he didn't know what that meant. He understood the heart of God was for His people, though the Lord had a hard path for them. He banked on the unchanging nature of God, that God wouldn't change His mind halfway through and smite Isaiah. Isaiah drew near to the Lord not because of his own faith nor what the Lord would do for him; He drew near because, even without knowing fully, he was betting on the gospel.

So even before we receive His mercy and rewards, while we're still in great need and can only trust Him a mustard seed amount, we are sure about one thing: Christ loves us. With repenting hearts and empty hands, raised in adoration, we approach God that He may supply mercy to our needy souls, strength to our tired bones, answers to our worn questions, and help to our confusing lives. He longs to give us this.

BE NEEDY

"If I can?" Jesus's voice rang in the father's ears, and he must have felt some sort of failure. He failed his son again because he didn't have enough faith. Faith. If only he had more *faith*. Then the father opened up his hands and declared to Jesus: "I believe, help my unbelief" (Mark 9:24).

The cry hung in the air.

I believe, help my unbelief.

He had reached the end of his rope, and he knew it. He could do no more, and even what he did wasn't enough. If Christ wasn't merciful here, the son would perish. If Christ didn't take the father's hand and lead him toward full faith, the father wouldn't make it either. The boy's father was completely needy before the Lord. He could not impress Christ with his faith nor his reasoning. He could only ask for help.

Behold, Christ came through. He drove out the spirit from the boy and returned him to his father. He didn't withhold mercy because the father struggled. In fact, even Christ's hard words of discipline are a mercy to the father. "If you can! All things are possible for the one who believes" (Mark 9:23). His rebuke wasn't ridicule; it was sanctification.

Before you go thinking that this story is about the father's faith, though, let's zoom out. Christ's discipline in this story is likely more meant for his disciples than this father. Look at the disciples' role in the story. They had been following Jesus for some time, now. Jesus sent them all out on a missionary journey where He gave them the power to drive out demons, heal diseases, and raise the dead (Matt. 10:5–7; Mark 6:7–13). They witnessed the miracles and heard the teachings of Christ. But they had also tasted of their own power, and they were noticing their own popularity gains.

Perhaps, subtly, they started to put faith in their own abilities rather than the power of Christ. They started to think the kingdom of God was like an earthly kingdom, one with a powerful ruler, wealth, and blessings. They got all mixed up when promoting the greatness of God and started to seek greatness in and of itself. They were fixated on being the best, first, and greatest so much so that Jesus humbled them over and over again in the chapters surrounding Mark 9. When they asked Christ why they couldn't drive out the demon, Christ replied, "This kind can only be driven out by prayer" (Mark 9:29). In other words, rely on God's power. They weren't trusting God, they were trusting themselves, and as these chapters in Mark go to show, we often just don't get it.

The disciples saw the Cross as defeat, but Christ says it is victory: "For whoever would save his life will lose it, but whoever loses his life for my sake and the gospel's will save it" (Mark 8:35).

The disciples were arguing about who was the greatest, but Jesus said: "If anyone would be first, he must be last of all and servant of all" (Mark 9:35).

The disciples were upset at people stealing their thunder, but Jesus said: "Do not stop him, for no one who does a mighty work in my name will be able soon afterward to speak evil of me" (Mark 9:39).

The disciples pushed away the insignificant children, but Jesus said, "Let the children come to me; do not hinder them, for to such belongs the kingdom of God" (Mark 10:14).

The disciples thought that wealth was a good goal, but Jesus said, "Children, how difficult it is to enter the kingdom of God! It is easier for a camel to go through the eye of a needle than for a rich person to enter the kingdom of God" (Mark 10:24–25).

The disciples were concerned with their placement in heaven, but Jesus said to them, "But whoever would be great among you must be your servant, and whoever would be first among you must be a slave of all. For even the Son of Man came not to be served but to serve and to give his life as a ransom for many" (Mark 10:43–44).

This section of Mark brings the disciples to a place where they recognize that Christ's kingdom is an upside-down one. It's not about how much they could do, how worthy they were, how many riches they had, what people thought of them, or even how successful their ministry was. It's not even about their ability to believe. Jesus was teaching them to be last, to be a servant, to be poor, and to *die* to self. He was teaching them not to put their faith in faith itself, or rather in their ability to have faith. He wanted their hearts. He wanted their scribbles of life, just like a father wants his daughter's pictures.

Thus, perhaps the hearts that truly needed to cry out "I believe, help my unbelief" were the disciples. Maybe Christ didn't heal the son because of the father's plea, but because He wanted to show to his disciples that *He was it*. He wanted to strengthen the disciples' faith by showing them that they could not do it themselves. They needed Him.

The boy's father in this miracle paves the way for the disciples and us to be needy before the Lord in faith, in all that we don't understand, and in all of the ways we trust something other than God. "I believe, help my unbelief" isn't a magic phrase that initiates healing in our lives. It is truly a call to surrender to the upside-down kingdom of God, where the first is last and the ruler is a servant. We don't get there through greatness; we get there through being needy before the Lord, like little children.

We need to stop hiding behind our spiritual strength. We are invited to stop only presenting the pleasing parts of our lives to the Lord. Sometimes the people most in need of the miracle aren't the ones who know they are sick but the ones who think that it is their responsibility to heal the others.

ASK FOR FAITH

The father in this passage paves the way for us not only to draw near and be needy, but to express that need to the Lord. He recognized his need and asked for greater faith. He was gutsy in his halfhearted belief, and that is what draws me into this story so much.

So here we are, needy and drawing near to God not because we are confident in ourselves but because we are confident in Christ. What do we do now?

Open your hands. Present that mustard seed of faith to the Lord and ask Him to take it, nurture it, and help it grow. Open your hands to receive His mercy and grace. Sit there in the struggle and let the Lord meet your needs.

But be bold enough to ask for it.

Ask, and it will be given to you; seek, and you will find; knock, and it will be opened to you. For everyone who asks receives, and the one who seeks finds, and to the one who knocks it will be opened.

—MATTHEW 7:7

You did not choose me, but I chose you and appointed you that you should go and bear fruit and that your fruit should abide, so that whatever you ask the Father in my name, he may give it to you.

—JOHN 15:16

And this is the confidence that we have toward him, that if we ask anything according to his will he hears us.

—1 JOHN 5:14

We do not ask a genie for our wishes to come true. We have something better. We have a Father who loves us and has full power to do what is best. When we draw near before Him in our need and ask for increased faith, He is faithful, and He will do it

—1 THESS 5:24

For the longest time, I never prayed for a husband. I felt as if that was forcing God's will or something (as if I have the power to do that). So instead of asking for a significant life change that I desired, I hid it from God. I pretended like I didn't need it. I dated and navigated singleness much on my own power. Again, I was trying to impress God.

It didn't turn out well. In fact, it wasn't until I was on my knees, aware of my need, and near to the Lord that I saw clearly. I saw that I could not do this alone, and that God wanted to *help* me in my need, even my small needs of loneliness and longing. In surrender before Him, I gained boldness to ask Him for my desires.

What do you want to ask the Lord for today? What desire seems too small, too cherished, or too big for the Lord? Ask Him. Perhaps in the asking, we will find that it is not for us. But perhaps in the asking we will find out what *is* for us, what is good and pleasing and perfect (Rom. 12:2).

I now regularly park my car at 11:30 p.m. and pour out my neediness before God. Only this time, I am not hiding behind my I-can-do-it attitude. I welcome the neediness. I see how it only points to God's ability to meet that need. Pride is put in place, and in humility, there is growth. Thus, my small percentage of faith increases as I draw near.

Maybe you're at a place where you aren't so sure about your faith. The father in Mark 9 wasn't either.

Draw near, be needy, and ask. Maybe you're at a place where you were overly confident in your own ability. That's where the disciples were. Draw near, be needy, and ask. The Lord isn't waiting for us to have it all together, so those who feel far from that are invited to come, and those who are desperately seeking to get it all together are invited to come.

Our needs are fully met in the Lord; they were that way all along.

GROWING ROOTS

▶ Do you struggle to be vulnerable to the Lord in seasons when you feel less-than-holy?

▶ What do you need today?

▶ How does the Lord meet that need?

Open Hands

Keeping our plans in open hands

CHAPTER SIX

Open Hands

A New Heart Posture

Letting go is both
freedom and fear;
freedom from what once had a hold on us
and fear that we will be left empty-handed.

So we let go, not of all things,
but of our desire to control all things,
and we hold tightly to Him who
holds all things together.

I t's about to get real here, folks.

Right before I turned twenty-five, the man I was starting to believe I would marry broke up with me over the phone for a reason I didn't understand. A dream I didn't even know that I cherished broke into pieces, and I was paralyzed as to how to handle it.

You may have been in a place like this, too. You may have had a dream dashed or a desire met with disaster.

You may have also been left at night with questions like "Why?" or "Why me and not them?"

You're in good company.

For a week, I didn't spend time alone at all. I went out of town twice, I worked a lot, and I spent time with family and friends. I listened to too many Taylor Swift songs. I cried at the gym. I did all the normal things. But I knew that what my soul needed was at least four uninterrupted hours with the Lord. Probably more.

The Monday after that eventful call, I locked myself in my room and prayed it out, examined the Scriptures, and sat there with the Lord in this disappointment. Out of that time, this book was born. I didn't know it at the time, but during those hours, something clicked in my heart, and I haven't been the same since. The Lord opened my hands that night, and not just because He took something from them, but because He humbled my heart to receive *Him*.

Cozy on in, because we're going to read an excerpt of what the Lord showed me that Monday night, locked up in my room, a gallon of ice cream waiting for me in the freezer (told you we were getting personal):

Father, you are faithful, compassionate, and all-knowing. I can trust that you know. I follow you, and you know where we are going.

You already know what I am going to puzzle out, but here it goes: when he started to break up with me, I felt it. I felt my grip tightening around our relationship and my own heart. It was no longer "keep your plans in open hands," it was "I can fix this." I puzzled and prayed and pondered how I could fix it. I knew it couldn't be over.

My grip was tight, fists that are only good for fighting. They grew stiff in their clenched position. I was determined just to be better, see more clearly, pray harder, get more insight, and figure out the perfect words to say. I wanted him back so badly, I forgot to trust You. I forgot to let You hold my hand throughout all of this, because fists can't hold a hand. They can't receive gifts, and the sad truth is that they clench air. They were my defense that left me weary. They were my instinct that exhausted my ability to worship.

I know that I have a lot of fight in me, but it is not enough to carry me there [a godly marriage]. I desire a place only You can carry me. How can You lift me up when my hands are closed to Your reach?

This was never my battle anyway.

This wasn't the first time I had thought about keeping my plans in open hands. My dad had told me that years before, when I was worried and concerned about many things (as I often do). I've said it often in my life as a twenty-something whose life changed every six months. In a journal from 2020, now water-damaged from when my house flooded, I wrote:

So instead of grasping at these desires, I open my hand, trusting, delighting, waiting. Even though I don't want to, even though this is counter to all I feel, I will trust the Lord. I will delight in the Lover of my soul. I will wait on the King of Kings...

I hold my hands open, full of desire to help another hand also at Your service. You placed these desires in my heart. It scared me to surrender these desires because I think by doing so, I am giving it all up, but rather I am gaining Christ.

All else is nothing compared to Christ.

Even throughout the relationship I lamented above, I would tell myself and the guy, "Open hands." My lips knew the practice, but my heart wasn't convinced. It is one thing to say "open hands" when they are full, but it is another thing entirely to say "open hands" when they seem rather empty. It was one thing to say "open hands" when things were going to plan, but when the plans that I held got taken away, where did I fall?

The day after I wrote that post-breakup entry, I sprained my ankle. It didn't seem like a big deal in the moment, but that injury lasted longer than any other injury I've had and made the upcoming months of healing, working, and serving a challenge just to physically do. It took six months for me to be able to sort of jump without pain, and as I teach ballet for a living, that was a struggle. It took several more months for me to get back to my usual intense exercise regime.

Additionally, I was going through a tough spot with my career. My business wasn't doing well, and I had a lot of decisions to make about how to proceed. I've always been more career-minded than relationship-minded, so this blow, though slower and less distinct, also really rattled me. The plans that I had made for my future no longer had a foundation, and the risks that I had taken weren't panning out. My financial situation worried me, and I reconsidered a lot of my decisions.

Then my best friend and roommate moved to Germany, and I felt more alone than I've perhaps ever felt (and I was homeschooled, so that's saying something). At the end of the day, there wasn't anyone checking up on me, and that kind of silence is loud.

"It's been pretty tough, hasn't it?" one lady at church said to me as we took care of the babies during the service. I had explained to her how the past couple of months have been, and she gave me a knowing look.

"When you say it all together like that, it does, doesn't it," I replied.

God plucked one thing after another from my hands. As my hands grew lighter, I could hear Him saying to me: *Do you trust me? Do you trust in who you know me to be rather than the gifts that I give you? Do you know that I will not forsake you? Do you trust that I am intimately familiar with your dreams and that I'm not teasing you? Will you step out of the boat and into the storm of life, fearlessly proclaiming the gospel even if it's not in the way that you expected? Will you really trust that my ways are better than your ways?*

A SMALL SIDE NOTE

This isn't a sob story about a rough season for me. I'm well aware that many of you reading this book today are going through situations I can't imagine, like the death of loved ones, long-term illnesses, unsaved family members, infertility, layoffs, and more. I haven't been there. I don't know what that's like.

Additionally, many of you are going through things that seem less-than but are still hard. Difficult bosses, challenging relationships, moving, the loss of friendships, or stressful weeks–those struggles are big, too. They are heavy, and the Lord wishes you to cast them on Him as well.

We can play the game of comparison with our struggles, either justifying our sorrow or hiding it away. I venture to say that we need not do either. Whatever is hard for you right now is *hard*. Even if someone has it harder or someone has it easier, let your burden be hard. And bring it to the Lord. Perspective is needed and useful, but don't sweep your pain under the rug because the person next to you has it worse.

After Hurricane Laura, a category five hurricane that caused historic damage to my area, tore through my town, everyone was asking everyone else how their house fared. Most of the time, people would reply, "Better than most." I almost felt cheated by that answer. Sister, we're all doing *worse* than most right now. I want the details. I want to know that your garage got hit by a tree and you have two nails in your tire and your corner bedroom's window is broken. Your damage isn't irrelevant because the next person's house is split in two.

So, wherever you are, whatever disappointments you face, "open hands" is for you. And if your struggles are more life-altering than mine, please forgive my limited experience.

Small side note over.

So, at the crossroads of desire and disappointment (a phrase borrowed from Emily P. Freeman's *Simply Tuesday* that I've never forgotten), I was given this phrase, "Keep your plans in open hands."[13] In the middle of a Monday night, my perspective shifted, and I've not held things the same since.

But what does that really mean?

I'd like to repeat a previous Corrie Ten Boom quote: "Hold everything in your hands lightly, otherwise it hurts when God pries your fingers open."[14] I like this phrasing, *holding lightly*. My friend Grace, a week before the breakup, told me, "I'm learning to surrender what I'd rather hold."

Are you acquainted with the book of Habakkuk? It is one of my favorite sections of Scripture because in

---

13 Emily P. Freeman, *Simply Tuesday* (Grand Rapids, MI: Revell, 2015), 181.

14 Corrie Ten Boom, "Quote by Corrie Ten Boom," Bible Portal, last accessed July 16, 2023, https://bibleportal. com/bible-quote/hold-everything-in-your-hands-lightly-otherwise-it-hurts-when-god-pries-your-fingers-open.

Habakkuk, we get to see someone show their plans to God, with all the hurt and confusion of the world, and learn to hold those desires with open hands, held up in worship rather than in anger.

HOLDING LOOSELY

Habakkuk takes place around 600 BC, about 100 years after the fall of the northern kingdom of Israel and shortly before the fall of the southern kingdom. Habakkuk had just experienced the reign of the good king Josiah and the hope of revival, only to be disappointed with the reign of Jehoiakim. The people then turned away from God. "The law is paralyzed, and justice never goes forth" (Hab. 1:4).

Habakkuk had a heart for justice and revival. He wanted to see his people turn to the Lord and cry out for help. He saw the failures of man and then turned to God. He had plans, and he waved them before the Lord in the hope that the Lord would act.

He had a plan.

And that is okay.

If we're going to keep our plans in open hands, we must first identify what those plans are. In my case, my plan is to get married and have a family. My plan is to see my business succeed and my friendships flourish. These aren't bad plans. Your plans are likely not bad plans, either. The Lord doesn't call us not to have plans, but rather to hold them loosely.

So much of our culture emphasizes letting things go, but I do not see that portrayed in the same manner in the Scriptures. Yes, we are called to cast our anxieties on Him. Yes, we are called to release our tight grip on life. Yes, we are called to a life of unabandoned trust in the Lord. However, this does not mean our lives are void of responsibilities and work. The Lord places many things in our hands, and it is our great joy and work to hold them.

Consider Elsa. (Yes, I am going to use Disney as an example. I own a business where I dress up as a princess and go to kids' birthday parties, so this feels appropriate.) When Disney first started creating Elsa, she was the villain. However, when the songwriters started working on her villain song, it turned into "Let It Go" and changed the trajectory of her character.[15] Elsa became a troubled lead character instead of the villain. It was the first time Disney had *two* female leads, Anna and Elsa.

---

15 Kirsten Acuna, "One Huge Change in the 'Frozen' Storyline Helped Make it a Billion-Dollar Movie," Business Insider, September 3, 2014, https://www.businessinsider.com/frozen-elsa-originally-villain-2014-9?op=1.

Disney expected the characters to garner the same amount of attention. Particularly, they anticipated Anna would gain more attention than she did. After all, Anna is the one who stays true to her character. She is the one who risks it for love. She is the one who saves the day in the end.

I can testify to the popularity of Elsa. I have a character based off Elsa's character for my business. This character is booked for parties almost every weekend, but my Anna-inspired character only goes out with the Ice Queen, and only about every third time, if that. Elsa is simply more popular than Anna. *By a lot.*

Why does Elsa steal the show?

Elsa attracts something in us that we all desire. She lets it go. She is free! She is strong! She is independent! And she looks fabulous while doing it.

The reality of this story, though, is that Elsa abandons her responsibilities when it gets sticky. Although "Let It Go" is truly an anthem, at its core, it is selfish. Elsa, at the cost of her sister and kingdom, runs away and causes a lot of hurt. What if Elsa, instead of either gripping tight in fear or letting it all go, learned to hold loosely? What if she could take off the gloves of risk-avoidant fear and learn to hold her responsibilities and relationships loosely?

Maybe she wouldn't have sung the power ballad that dads everywhere *adore*, but I think she would have spared her family and kingdom a lot of trouble, and certainly a lot of ice. (Thank you for bearing with my Disney-nerd analogy and rant about Elsa.)

For my heart, to hold the pain of a breakup loosely meant learning to love my ex differently. It meant obeying the Lord by praying for him and accepting the changes in our relationship. It meant not clinging to my old dreams. Additionally, holding loosely meant not giving up on the idea that God would provide someone in my life to marry. I can still hold that dream without choking it.

NOT ME

Habakkuk tells God his complaint, his plan, and his disappointments, and then he waits to see what God's response will be. He plays his hand, confident that he is right, and watches to see what God will do.

God's answer? "For I am doing a work in your days that you would not believe if I told. For behold, I am raising up the Chaldeans, that bitter and hasty nation" (Hab. 1:5-6).

That is not what Habakkuk expected. God, in response to Habakkuk's lament over Israel, reveals to Habakkuk that the Chaldeans (the Babylonians) will soon rule over Israel. The justice that Habakkuk longed for is coming, but only to be replaced by greater injustice. God is working a plan that is so far outside of what Habakkuk was thinking that Habakkuk wouldn't even believe it if God told it to him.

Naturally, Habakkuk complains again, voicing his concern about the Babylonians and how they mercilessly kill and treat people like animals. Then he awaits the Lord again.

The Lord's response this time? "For still the vision awaits its appointed time; it hastens to the end- it will not lie. If it seems slow, wait for it; it will surely come; it will not delay" (Hab. 2:2-3).

First, note that God doesn't correct Habakkuk's questions or rebuke his concerns. God listens to Habakkuk's complaint and gives space to his confusion. Then God corrects Habakkuk's plan and the timing of his expectations, giving him a new plan and timeline. We see in the rest of chapter two that God's heart is also for justice and revival, but that it will come in a different way than Habakkuk desired and in a timeline that Habakkuk will only see in part.

The answer to Habakkuk's cry for salvation was a "yes," but Habakkuk would see it only from afar. It wouldn't happen the way Habakkuk desired. He was about to go through a terrible time of capture and despair. He was going to see suffering, injustice, and famine. This book, unlike other prophetic works, isn't so much a warning to the people or a call to repentance as much as it is a lament.

The timeline didn't favor Habakkuk at all. The outcome was not about how well Habakkuk asked for rescue. It was not about how pure Habakkuk's heart was. It was not about how skilled a prophet Habakkuk was. Despite the name, the book of Habakkuk is not about Habakkuk.

And that, my friends, is the best part.

Keeping our plans in open hands is remembering that it is not about us, either. It's not about how good or pure our plans are. It's not about how productive, loving, or godly we are. We perhaps think that we can control our lives, and this makes us hesitate to open our tight grip on life, but we only fool ourselves. We can control life as well as we can grasp sand in our hands. We can hold it as tightly as we want to, but it's slipping through either way. Our reluctance to live a life joyfully surrendered to the Lord doesn't intercept His plans for us; it only makes it all the more painful when He pries our little fingers from around the remnants of sand we thought we held.

It is better to remember that our stories are not about us. Like Habakkuk, we must remember that our ability to execute the plan doesn't mean that the plan is going to work out. The Lord is doing something bigger than us and our desires, and He will not delay. He is using us for good, even if that good isn't in our plan.

In my instance, I thought that if I could just be perfect, respond perfectly, and say the perfect thing, then the guy would come back to me, my job would succeed, and I would be healed. That pressure crushed me. More than that, it blocked God out of the picture. It was, as I said, my instinct that exhausted my ability to worship. A close-handed life is one of isolation and pride. *I can do it. I can fix it.* We aren't meant to carry that load.

You aren't meant to carry the load of being perfect in your career. You aren't meant to carry the burden of being the perfect mother. You aren't meant to control the attitudes of your friends and family toward Christ. You can't bear the pressures of knowing where life is headed. You aren't meant to keep all the sand in your hand.

Life isn't in our control, but it is in God's control, and we are to trust Him. There it is—*trust*. An open-handed life is one of trust in who the Lord is and that He will give us what is best, even if that goes against our plans and timelines.

We trust that when He takes away the possibility of marriage for the time being, it is glorious and for our good.

We trust that when the test comes back with bad results, He isn't absent.

We trust that when relationships are hard and ever-changing, He remains the same.

We trust that in the constant strain of life, He is gentle and lowly.

We trust *Him*.

When I start to close my grip around my life and seek control over worship, I know that I need to sit at the feet of Jesus. I'm becoming worried and concerned about many things, but few things are needed—indeed, only one (Luke 10:42). Open hands actively choose what is *best*, and that takes time. That takes real work in our hearts. It takes real work to turn off the sad song and play worship music. It takes real work to persevere in your job even though you don't want to be there. It takes real work to continue to love on your family even after a decade of them not choosing Christ. It takes real work to rejoice when your friend has her third kid and you're still waiting. It takes real work to open up our hands around our lives and leave them open to God's plan. This work is hard because it is *humbling,* a reminder that it is not about us.

YET I WILL REJOICE

Keeping our plans in open hands is to worship freely. Worship takes our eyes off of ourselves, our worries, and our disappointments. Worship orients our hearts around the character of God.

Matt Redman said, "The heart of God loves a persevering worshiper who, though overwhelmed by many troubles, is overwhelmed even more by the beauty of God."[16]

Habakkuk ends, in my opinion, with one of the most powerful prayers in scripture.

> Though the fig tree should not blossom, nor fruit be on the vines, the produce of the olive fail and the fields yield no food, the flock be cut off from the fold and there be no herd in the stalls, yet I will rejoice in the LORD; I will take joy in the God of my salvations. GOD, the LORD, is my strength; he makes my feet like the deer's; he makes me tread on my high places.
>
> —HABAKKUK 3:17-19

---

16 Matt Redman, *The Unquenchable Worshipper: Coming Back to the Heart of Worship* (Delight, AK: Gospel Light Publishing, 2001), 24.

I adore Habakkuk because, at the end of the day, God told him *no*. Habakkuk did not get to see his desires come to fruition. He didn't get twice the things that he lost, like Job (Job 42:10). He didn't get the answers or the reason why. Habakkuk lived in the middle of the story, the dark before the light, and in *that* period he found it good to rejoice in the Lord.

He was about to lose his kingdom and go through hell, yet he sings praise to the Lord. He was told that vicious people were coming, yet he chooses joy in the Lord over anger or fear. What, then, could man do to Habakkuk that he would lose his confidence? In the losing, he rejoices. Habakkuk stands on the most solid ground at the end of this book of questioning. This gives me courage to keep my plans open to the Lord, because even if nothing turns out the way I wanted, the Lord is my strength. He will give me the ability to navigate that path. He will preserve me. He will be faithful, for that is who He is.

Timothy Keller, in *Walking with God in Pain and Suffering,* elaborates on the strength of choosing to worship in the hardship: "We can choose to serve God just because he is God. In the darkest moments we feel we are getting absolutely nothing out of God or out of our relationship with him. Be what if *then*- when it does not seem to be paying or benefitting you at all—

you continue to obey, pray to, and seek God . . . ? If we do that- we are finally learning to love God for himself, and not for his benefits . . . We'll find new fortitude, unflappability, poise, and peace in the face of difficulty. The coal is becoming a diamond."[17]

* * *

Let's go back to that Monday night, locked up in my room a week after a breakup.

I started that night angry, sad, and confused. I expected to cry. I expected bitterness and grief. Instead, I found Jesus. Here is the ending of that journal entry:

So against my feelings, and in a messy, imperfect way, here I am.

I open my hands.

I change the position of my heart from trying to figure it all out to sitting at the feet of the One who has all things figured out. I turn from bitterness, anxiety, self-reliance, anger, insecurity, doubt, and pride. I make my strategy not to know why he did this, but to know how to best worship the Lord in this.

I open my hands.

---

17 Timothy Keller, *Walking With God In Pain and Suffering* (New York, NY: Penguin Books, 2013), 249.

Open hands are a position of worship. They are an invitation for someone to pray with me. They are ready to receive, and they are ready to give. You give and You take away—praise Your name forever. Open hands are trusting. They are vulnerable. They are on display. They are ready.

I open my hands.

My friends, let me impress upon you what my heart needs to hear today as well: opening your hands isn't choosing the short end of the stick. Opening your hands isn't settling for the hard. Opening your hands to the Lord is hard, yes, but it is actually resting in the *best*. It's a diamond bracelet instead of the stick. It is powerful. An open-handed life is not about changing the outcome of our lives but about changing the position of our hearts.

Habakkuk may have seen the dry part of the story. He may have walked through the valley of evil, but God was looking ahead to a better Savior. Habakkuk, by submitting to God's will, was also looking forward to the Christ. We established that the book of Habakkuk isn't about Habakkuk. Who, then, is it about? It is about Jesus. The longings he had for justice? Satisfied on the Cross. The burden he had for his people? Fulfilled by Immanuel, God with us.

A study of Habakkuk by Kristen Schmucker said, "If Habakkuk could have seen from his watchtower far into the future on the nearby hill of Calvary, he would have known the answer to every question that burdened his heart that day."[18]

Opening your hands isn't settling for hard; it is receiving the gospel, which is best. Your pain and your valley aren't about you. They are about Jesus. Because He came and opened His hands at the Cross, we can open our hands to His will. How amazing that our lives, our suffering, our dreams, and our struggles get to be folded into the story of the gospel!

Let me encourage you, friend, to spend time right now in prayer. Get on your knees. Like Habakkuk, ask your questions. Literally open up your hands and stare at them. What are you holding close that He's calling you to surrender? What plan of yours needs to be examined through the will of God? Who are you putting in a position in your life that only God can fill? What do you think you must control when you must first realize *God* controls? What sorrow haunts your soul? What question never leaves? What pride in your ministry do you cling to?

---

18 Kristin Schmucker, *Even If* (Spring, TX: The Daily Grace Company, 2017), 33.

We are urged to bring these things and more before the Lord in our open hands. Identify them. Be specific. And one by one, know that the Lord can handle each and every one of these fears, situations, burdens, sorrows, and desires. Place them in His hands. Release the worries, the strategies, and the expectations. Take on, instead, a great rejoicing in the finished work of the gospel in your life and today's involvement with God's perfect plan. His hands can hold the whole world, and no grain of sand leaves His palm without His intent.

GROWING ROOTS

▶ Which plans you are gripping tightly today?

▶ What would it mean to hold them loosely?

▶ How can you rejoice in the Lord today, even if things aren't the way you thought they would be?

CHAPTER SEVEN

He Gives and He Takes Away

Trusting God With the Worst-Case Scenarios

Why do I pick at my scabs?
It is as if I think that if I pick at the
tough
brittle
places they will be as new again.
I'm uneasy until everything is smooth,
but picked-at scabs don't heal;
they scar.
I think that by picking I'm in
control,
but I'm not in control of the
hurt or the healing;
the only thing my anxious hands
can do is scar.
So I'm learning to leave my hands
open,
even though there are still
scabs on my heart.

"It isn't fair."

How many times do those words come out of our mouths? When we are met with disappointments, disasters, and distress, something in us cries out, "It's not supposed to be this way!" It rubs against our souls and brings up some tough questions.

One of the biggest challenges to living an open-handed life is the sneaky fear that surrender means suffering unfairly. We think to pry our fingers away from our carefully crafted plans and dreams means to watch them all be torn in two by a tornado (more on that tornado thing later). We fear that perhaps God won't treat us as He should, or rather, how we want Him to treat us.

I don't know about you, but when I think about opening my hands, I think about accepting worst-case scenarios. It's one thing to surrender your love life to God, and it's another thing to be faithful in singleness your whole life when all your friends are married. It's one thing to place in open hands your healing, and it's another thing to face the reality of a lifetime of health struggles with hope. It's one thing to trust God with your family's spiritual health, but it's another thing to trust the Lord when you lose someone who maybe didn't love the Lord.

So, let's go there. Let's visit the worst-case scenario and see if it is still worth it to trust God.

From August 2020 to August 2021, four natural disasters hit my hometown. You heard me right, *four*. We started off strong with category four storm Hurricane Laura, who tore through Southwest Louisiana with winds up to 140 miles per hour. It was the worst storm we'd ever seen, comparable to Hurricane Katrina, which hit New Orleans some fifteen years prior. The landscape of our city changed. Trees were barren, and branches littered the ground. Homes were split in half by limbs, torn through with tornados, and flooded either from the ground up or from holes in roofs. Many people moved. Many businesses didn't make it. Some homes, going on four years later, are still under construction.

A month later, Hurricane Delta came through, and although the winds were less severe, the flooding was worse. Some people had just finished repairs to their homes from Laura when Delta reversed all their progress. Three months later, Ice Storm Yuri burst pipes everywhere for the ill-prepared Southern homes. I knew of a home that finished Laura repairs just days before the ice storm ruined the home with flooding again. Almost four months after that, what started as a normal day ended with twelve inches of rain, more than both Hurricane Laura and Hurricane Delta brought combined. Because the drainage was clogged due to the storms, countless homes were destroyed, including mine. I had just settled into my new home, when the home, my new furnishings, and my beloved car were covered with a foot of water. I'll never forget crying on my parents' couch after my landlord FaceTimed me to show my baby blue convertible Bug, ruined. I was pretty dramatic.

To add to that, in the fall of 2022, a random tornado passed through the area, and it divided my childhood home in two with my mom and sister still inside. Thankfully, they were safe, but it was a traumatic day. We call the tornado our bonus fifth disaster during the year of all things bad weather.

If anyone is in a position to cry out, "It isn't fair," it is my hometown, and specifically my family.

If anyone in the Bible has to wrestle with the unfairness of life, it is Job. If I'm being honest, I tend to avoid studying Job. It seems hard. It seems like if I study Job then my life might mirror Job's, and I don't want that. But threaded throughout these chapters is the anchored grace of the Lord. It isn't about what Job can and cannot do. It isn't about what is fair and unfair. It is about the Lord, and *He is good*. But I'm getting ahead of myself. Let's learn about an open-handed posture in the face of unfair suffering through Job's worship, Job's righteousness, and the Lord's response.

JOB'S WORSHIP

This guy is the prime example of how the Lord can empty our hands. Job once held more wealth than he knew what to do with. In fact, he was the *greatest*. His hands were full of the blessings of the Lord, from his ten children to his 7,000 sheep. Not only that, but Job, in his wealth, did not turn from the Lord. He was "blameless and upright" (Job 1:1).

But then Lord pried open Job's hand in a very dramatic way, perhaps the most dramatic way. In one swoop, the Lord made a point of emptying Job's hands. Job's servant tells him that the oxen and donkeys are gone. He's the only one left to tell the tale. Another servant runs up and exclaims that the sheep and servants are burned with fire from heaven. He's the only one left to tell the tale. Another servant laments that the camels have been stolen. He's the only one left to tell the tale.

> While he was yet speaking, there came another and said, "Your sons and daughters were eating . . ."
>
> —Job 1:18

Right here, I feel it. I feel Job's stomach turn. His heart rate, which has risen through the roof, halts. He hasn't even grasped the pain of losing his livelihood when his family . . . oh, it couldn't be . . . not his children.

> . . . and drinking wine in their oldest brother's house, and behold, a great wind came across the wilderness and struck the four corners of the house, and it fell upon the young people, and they are dead . . .
>
> —Job 1:19

Here I imagine that Job doesn't hear the rest of the servant's report. Of course it ends the same way as the other reports of bad news: "I alone have escaped to tell you" (Job 1:19).

The servants' eyes followed Job as he arose, tore his robe, shaved his head, fell on the ground, and worshiped. *That* my friends, is the correct posture after the Lord takes it all from our hands. Before a word is spoken, Job worships. Before the questions are asked, Job adores the Lord. Before the grief sets in, Job bows down low.

His instinct was to worship.

"Naked I came from my mother's womb, and naked I shall return. The Lord gave, and the Lord has taken away, blessed be the name of the LORD" (Job 1:21–22). In all this, Job did not sin or charge God with wrong.

We should all be majorly impressed with this response. Mine is usually a lot of crying to my mom first, like when I lost my car. Mine is usually a lot of questions first, like when I broke my foot. It usually takes me much longer to arrive at this posture, the one that Job went to instinctively. This requires consistent practice. Job had already instilled the discipline of submitting to the Lord, so when disaster struck, he was ready to fall to his knees. He had practiced an open-handed posture with his life prior to catastrophe, so he was better prepared, even if no one can be fully prepared for anything in life.

It doesn't get better from here, unfortunately. Next up are the sores, the painful, distracting, terrible sores. Yet again, Job doesn't blame God. Even when his wife throws in the towel, he bows before God's sovereignty and superiority. Job's response to God taking everything away from him shows us that when we're faced with disappointment, disaster, or distress, we *must* worship the Lord. We must bow before Him, with many or few words.

Job didn't question fairness or voice regret in trusting the Lord. He didn't beg or bargain or belittle. He wasn't bitter. He sat in the sorrow and worshiped, and we have much to learn from that.

JOB'S RIGHTEOUSNESS

Now it gets tricky. For although Job's initial response is commendably great, the aftermath is harder. It is one thing to respond to life's sorrows in the moment, but the true challenge to living open-handed is the next day. And the day after that. And the day after that. The surrendered attitude of Job's initial response is harder to find in his other laments. They are messy. They are often words for the wind (Job 6:26; 8:2–3; 15:2; 16:3; 35:16), meaning that they are words spoken from grief rather than truth.

In the days after Hurricane Laura, everyone stayed strong. People posted #SWLAStrong. There was this urgency to respond well because if you didn't, water would keep coming into your ceiling and the roads would keep having limbs block them. But the weeks, months, and years that followed the storm are what truly challenged the grit of my community. When insurance companies didn't respond. When the contractor didn't show. When it had been six months and the part you needed was still on backorder. *That's* when it's hard to respond well.

Let's take a step back. Before the trials of Job, we see a bit of closed hands. It says that "His sons used to go and hold a feast in the house of each one on his day, and they would send and invite their three sisters to eat and drink with them. 5 And when the days of the feast had run their course, Job would send and consecrate them, and he would rise early in the morning and offer burnt offerings according to the number of them all. For Job said, "It may be that my children have sinned, and cursed[a] God in their hearts." Thus Job did continually." (Job 1:4-5).

I'm not to know the heart of Job here, but I wonder if this extra-careful righteousness, this rising early just in case they sinned, was a sign of Job's hands tightening around his gifts. Fearful that these blessings wouldn't last forever, did he seek to control not only his own righteousness but the righteousness of his children? Certainly we see here that Job was meticulously righteous, to the point of pride, as we see throughout the book.

Might I ask here if Job trusted in God here or his own ability to rise early in the morning and purify his children? Did Job have his fingers flat to the goodness of the Lord, or were they closed around his wealth and happiness? I'm not sure we get the answer to these exact questions, but we can relate to the struggle. When things are going well, we want to preserve that. We want to shelter the oasis of blessings from the storms. We want to build homes that are indestructible to any hurricane.

We pray that we get to keep them. We are careful to do right in case the consequences of *not* doing right are hard to bear.

This only works on the assumption that good people get good things and bad people get bad things. This careful self-righteousness hinges on the framework of a works-based life. It begs the question, "Is life fair?"

Back and forth, Job and his friends puzzle out the *why* of this suffering. Job becomes increasingly confident, and his friends become increasingly foolish. Job tip toes away from despair and inches towards the gospel, even though he doesn't know what that is yet. He shows this in verses like:

Though he slay me, I will hope in him.

—Job 13:15

Twisted in these pleas and rebukes is pride, confusion, fear, and a tight grip on Job's own righteousness. Job's friends attempt to understand the world through actions and consequences. Something bad happened to Job, thus Job must have done something bad. Now, remember that Job and his friends live pre-gospel. They don't have the illustration of grace via the Cross before their eyes. God operated in a way that was more reflective of actions and consequences, but there was yet grace. Job's friends weren't necessarily *wrong* about many things, but they missed the point with verses like:

> If you are pure and upright, surely then he will rouse himself for you.
>
> — JOB 8:6

> If iniquity is in your hand, put it far away, and let not injustice dwell in your tents. Surely then you will lift up your face without blemish; and you will be secure and will not fear.
>
> —JOB 11:14-15

Job, on the other hand, defends his righteousness with vigor. He becomes increasingly confident that he didn't do anything to deserve this catastrophe with verses like these:

> Through I am in the right, my own mouth would condemn me . . . I am blameless.
>
> —JOB 9:20-21

> There is no violence in my hands, and my prayer is pure.
>
> —JOB 16:17

To top it off, Job so much as says that he is clenching his own righteousness in 27:6: "I hold fast my righteousness and will not let it go; my heart does not reproach me for any of my days."

He becomes stronger and his answers longer as his friends' answers become shorter until Zophar doesn't even reply. Job isn't wrong here. He didn't deserve what happened to him. He did do what is right before the Lord. But perhaps here, Job also misses the point.

Keller says, "The world is too fallen and deeply broken to divide into a neat patten of good people having good lives and bad people having bad lives . . . The presumption of spiritual entitlement dooms its bearers to a life of confusion when things in life inevitably go wrong."[19] Although there is much to admire about Job's response to suffering, he wasn't perfect. He struggled to keep his plans in open hands, too. He struggled not to be spiritually entitled, and I think keeping that in mind helps us interpret the Lord's answer more clearly.

THE LORD'S RESPONSE

Then the Lord answers.

Who is this that darkens counsel by works without knowledge? . . . Where were you when I laid the foundation of the earth? Tell me, if you

---

19 Timothy Keller, *Walking with God Through Pain and Suffering* (New York, NY: Penguin Books, 2013) 114–15.

have understanding . . . Have you commanded the morning since your days began? . . .Can you send forth lightings, that they may go and say to you, "Here we are"? . . . Do you know when the mountain goats give birth? . . . Do you give the horse his might? . . . Shall a faultfinder contend with the Almighty?

—JOB 38:2, 4, 12, 35; 39:1,19; 40:2

At first, the Lord's answer seems harsh. After all, Job has been through a lot. He has a lot of valid questions. He has so much hurt. Doesn't the Lord know that? Why does the Lord ignore the questions and instead place before Job His own majesty? Why does the Lord boast in His greatness after bringing Job so low?

Look again.

Job is asking *why,* but God says *who.* Himself. God doesn't explain the behind-the-scenes conversations that are happening. God doesn't give answers, a feeling, or an outcome right away. He demands that Job look upon who He is.

He is beyond time. He is all-knowing. He is Creator. He is sustainer. He is caring. He is sovereign. He is mighty. He is Lord.

Thus, we see again that Job is called to trust not in what God gives him, but in *who God is*. God rebukes the ways that Job tried to make his own righteousness the answer. God rebukes Job's friends who try to make Job's wickedness the answer. God instead makes Himself great.

That is the most merciful thing the Lord could have done for Job. The greatest need for Job in his suffering was to better know the character of God. The answer to Job's soul's questions wasn't to receive gifts from the Lord but to receive the majestic character of the Lord Himself. The resting point for Job's sorrow wasn't even a comforting embrace from the Lord (although He is our Comforter) but a firm redirection to the Lord's glory, and this is what was best for Job. How do I know that was best for Job? Because that is what the Lord did.

At the end, Job responds: "I know that you can do all things, and that no purpose of yours can be thwarted. 'Who is this that hides counsel without knowledge?' Therefore I have uttered what I did not understand, things too wonderful for me, which I did not know" (Job 42:2-3).

At the end, Job not only opens his hands regarding his possessions, his family, and his health, he has open hands about his own righteousness and understanding.

Through the Lord's work, Job sees that he doesn't see things clearly. He comes before the Lord needy instead of sufficient. He knows—in fact, he *sees* that all he has is found in who God is (Job 42:5). That is more than enough, more abundant than we will ever understand.

Here we see that Job, after the wrestling and questioning, comes out the other side with an even firmer trust in the Lord. The man went down the path of worst-case scenarios and deemed it *worth it* when deciding to trust God.

You probably know the end of the story—the Lord blessed Job more at the end than in the beginning. He ended with twice the sheep, twice the camels, twice the donkeys. He had ten more children and is revered in the land again. But this isn't the point, the point is that Job's story points to the Lord.

Remember the year of bad weather for SWLA? Well, through these storms and trials, I have seen the resiliency and compassion of my neighbors more than ever before. After the tornado hit my parent's house, I couldn't even park my car on their street because it was so full of helping hands. We needed a moving van? Suddenly there were two. Were we hungry? Chick-fil-a dropped from the sky like manna.

Through the disasters, the gospel was shared. Samaritan's Purse stayed at my church for two years after Hurricane Laura, building fifty homes and sharing the love of Christ in powerful, tangible ways. I got to witness one home as they finished, and I'll never forget how close I felt to heaven in that moment. I do not pretend to justify or make light of the suffering, but I have seen firsthand how it was still somehow and undeniably *good*.

Then there's Audrey Lane, my baby blue convertible Volkswagen Beetle. She was my personality in a car, and everyone knew who was driving around town every Sunday afternoon with the top down and the music loud when they saw her. My car somehow managed to not get damaged during both hurricanes, but in the unexpected flood, Audrey died. And I cried.

There were three other cars like mine in the area (and I knew I would need to buy locally and quickly). What are the odds that the lady thirty minutes north of me would sell her baby blue convertible Beetle the day I lost mine? But there it was, on Facebook Marketplace, the night I was crying on my parent's couch over a car.

Two days later, we bought Audrey Hope, my second baby blue convertible Bug. She is actually better than my previous car, but my favorite thing about her is that to this day, I remember the faithfulness of the Lord as displayed through finding and buying this car. He didn't have to provide like that, but He did. He showed me that He might take some things from my hands, and it might not be fair, but it's also not fair that I would find my exact car on Facebook Marketplace that night I lose mine.

I'm learning to love the way life isn't fair.

* * *

When we are fearful that surrendering our lives to the Lord guarantees suffering, we can look to Job. He counted it worth it. The Lord was still good to him, even in the suffering. He didn't know the answers or the outcome, but he saw the Lord, and that was so much more than fair.

Let Psalm 145 be our prayer, as we open our hands to the Lord, who opens His hands to us. Just like Job, this psalm points our souls to the character of God. He is righteous. He is majestic. He is glorious. He is *near*. He is *Savior*. He is *kind*. With God's character before us, we are invited to call on him in trust. We are compelled to cry out to Him who saves. Life gives us many questions, laments, and sorrows. Bring those to the Lord. He hears you. He satisfies you out of His hand. He fulfils your desires. He preserves you. Let this psalm give us confidence to call on Him when we are falling or when we fear the fall.

> The LORD is faithful in all his words
> and kind is all his works.
> The LORD upholds all who are falling
> And raises up all who are bowed down.
> The eyes of all look to you
> And you give them their food in due season.
> You open your hand;
> You satisfy the desire of every living thing.
> The LORD is righteous in all his ways
> And kind in all his works.
> The LORD is near to all who call on him,
> To all who call on him in truth.
> He fulfils the desires of those who fear him;
> He also hears their cry and saves them.
> The LORD preserves all who love him,
> But all the wicked he will destroy.
> My mouth will speak the praise of the LORD,
> And let all flesh bless his holy name forever and ever.

—PSALM 145:13-21

GROWING ROOTS

▶ Do you fear that surrendering to the Lord means He is going to take away things you love?

▶ How does the character of God address that fear?

▶ How can you practice worship in your life so that it is your instinct in times of trouble?

CHAPTER EIGHT

The Hands of God

He Holds Us Tightly in His Hands

Five years old and the crowds swarm in.
Panic creeps up
till you find Dad's hand.

Fifteen years old and the world gets big.
You feel left behind
till you find a friend's hand.

Twenty-five years old and life gets hard.
Decisions scream loud
till you find his hand.

Thirty-one years old and it's a bit too much.
You need some rest
till you find her little hand

Sixty years old and you begin to wonder.
Did you do it right
till you find his hand.

There's something about a hand in yours
that makes life safe again.
There's something about fingers interlocked
that changes the locks on your heart.

> My sheep hear my voice, and I know them, and
> they follow me. I give them eternal life, and they
> will never perish, and no one will snatch them
> out of my hand. My Father, who has given them
> to me, is greater than all, and no one is able to
> snatch them out of the Father's hand.
>
> —John 10:27-29

I have an ESV journaling Bible that has a few little
sketches of keywords and things that the Lord has put
on my heart throughout the years. The pressure to write
perfect things using perfect pens can stifle a regular
habit of journaling, but the little sketches I do have are
precious to me. Those colorful little words and pictures
have stuck in my brain. I associate certain passages with
what is on the margins of my Bible, and no passage more
than John 10.

My favorite margin journal doodle is found on the
bottom left corner of the Gospel of John in chapter 10.
It's a picture of a giant hand holding a sheep, and over
the hand is one word: "unsnatchable." I know it's not a
word, but perhaps it should be. Perhaps it is a powerful
word.

Unsnatchable.

My vision with this drawing is to imagine a little
sheep in the hands of a giant. The sheep tries to run out

of the giant's hands and reaches the fingertips—almost there—only to have the fingers fold over and place the sheep right back where he started. Again and again, the little sheep tries to leave the giant's hands, but they keep placing that sheep exactly where he needs to be, in the middle of his palm. The wind may blow hard and seek to blow the sheep off the hand, but the hand shelters the sheep from the wind. A bird may swoop in and seek to pluck the sheep from the hand, but the hand is more powerful than the bird. The hand holding the sheep is a sure refuge and strong fortress (Ps. 144:2).

This image of a sheep safe in God's hand was absolutely solidified by this video I found years ago. Simply search "Sheep Stuck in Tire Swing."[20] Please take thirty seconds to watch this; you won't regret it.

When I saw this video for the first time several years ago, I showed it to everyone I knew. Not only did it make me chuckle, but it was an exact illustration of what John 10 says. We are like that sheep, firmly planted in God's hand like we're stuck in a tire swing. We can try to out-sin, out-perform, out-plan, or out-grow God's hand, but we end up right back in the center of it. Dreams, disasters, and disappointments may disorient us, but He comforts us even when we look for comfort elsewhere.

20 The Sun, "Sheep STUCK in a rope swing," YouTube, August 19, 2018, https://youtu.be/TtC666biAUY.

When we surrender our dreams, plans, and hopes to God, we are not left empty-handed; we are left in the middle of God's hands. When we turn our eyes from what we think should be or what we want things to be, then we can see what is true: God has been holding us all this time. An open-handed life of trust in God works only because we are first in the Father's hands.

You are unsnatchable.

For he is our God, and we are the people of his pasture, and the sheep of his hand.

—PSALM 95:7

HIS HANDS PROTECT US

I do not have strong hands. They are, as my sisters say, unusually small and cold. When I first started to work out, I was so proud of my little callouses. However, my weak grip strength limited my overall ability to perform. Although my legs could handle heavier lifts, my hands couldn't. Hand strength may seem insignificant, but in order to deadlift 200 pounds, I have to be able to grip it. The smallest weakness has been my downfall time and time again.

I wonder if, when we are trusting our lives to God, we question His grip strength. We aren't questioning His strength in general, but rather His ability to provide for our dreams, disappointments, and disasters. It seems scary to fall into the hands of God if we doubt their ability to catch us. Therefore, we keep a few plans to ourselves. We make a few choices without asking God first. We push through some situations without surrendering to God, not because we don't think Him strong, but maybe just not in this small way.

A familiar verse shines some light on this subject.

Humble yourselves, therefore, under the mighty hand of God so that at the proper time he may exalt you, casting all your anxieties on him, because he cares for you.

—1 PETER 5:6–7

Peter says that God's hand is *mighty*. He doesn't say that God's hand is gentle (though it is). He doesn't say that God's hand is comforting (though it is). He says that God's hand is *mighty*.

I write this in Utah right now, cozied up in a little lodge. Yesterday, I stood on top of 2,000-foot cliffs at Horseshoe Bend. There were tiny people at the bottom of the cliff camping, but I had to squint my eyes to see them. I was quite aware that one wrong step could send me flying for a minute or two and crashing the next. The astronomical size of the cliff humbled me. It made me seem so small because the cliff was so mighty. It is hard to humble yourself under something underwhelming. We must first open our eyes to the majesty of God before we can learn to humble ourselves and thus be freed to cast our cares on Him.

Consider the role of humility in this truth spelled out in 1 Peter 5:6–7. "Casting all your anxiety on him" is a *dependent* clause, hanging off of "humble yourselves." When we think we are hot stuff and can handle life in our own power, we aren't going to toss the ball to Jesus. When we think that perhaps we know better than He does about a situation, we aren't going to ask for advice. However, we are called to humility— admitting that we are not strong enough, wise enough, or caring enough to navigate our lives.

The plans that you thought were perfect? They aren't. The job that seemed meant for you? It might not be. The boyfriend you wanted to marry? Maybe not. Surrendering our best efforts to God is humbling.

Why would we risk that? Why would we cast it all off? Because God's hands are mighty. His ways are better. His thoughts are higher. Unlike our meager abilities to control our lives, God has infinite ability. His hands are not weak.

This is the purpose that is purposed concerning the whole earth, and this is the hand that is stretched out over all the nations. For the Lord of hosts has purposed, and who will annul it? His hand is stretched out, and who will turn it back?

—Isaiah 14:26-27

The hand of the Lord holds all life (Job 12:10), set the plagues in place (Ex. 9:3), brought the Israelites out of Egypt (Deut. 5:15), punished the unfaithful Israelites (Judg. 2:15), caused the church to grow (Acts 11:21), and more. The hand of the Lord is often depicted in Scripture in terms of battles won or lost. Either the hand of the Lord was against a people or for a people, and that was the determining factor of their victory. It didn't matter the army's strength or numbers. The only thing that mattered was the hand of the Lord.

This is a fearsome thing, the mighty hand of the Lord. In contemporary Christian culture, I don't hear much about fearing the Lord. We are eager to talk about the comforting hand of the Lord, but not so much the powerful one, unless that power is directed at getting rid of our problems. However, God is not powerful so that our problems go away. God is powerful. End of sentence. It's simply not about us. He is fall-on-the-ground-in-awe powerful. He is stand-at-the edge-of-a-cliff-in-awe majestic. We shouldn't brush past looking at the glorious, mighty hand of the Lord because we'd rather peer into His goodness instead. They are one and the same. The same hand that mightily enacted the plagues against Egypt also guided the Israelites in the desert. The same hand that opposed the Philistines to the point of destruction raised Christ from the dead.

We are clearly called to fear the Lord in Scripture: "The fear of the LORD is the beginning of knowledge" (Prov. 1:7). "And now, Israel, what does the LORD your God require of you, but to fear the LORD your God, to walk in all his ways, to love him, to serve the LORD your God with all your heart and with all your soul" (Deut. 10:12).

Even Christ feared the LORD: "And the Spirit of the Lord shall rest upon him, the Spirit of wisdom and understanding, the Spirit of counsel and might, the Spirit of knowledge and the fear of the LORD" (Isa. 11:2).

This fear isn't a run-away-scared kind of fear, though. It is a reverent knowledge and humble submission to God's god-ness. When we submit to His rule we see our smallness in the shadow of His greatness, and this is the best place for us to be. Consider the words of 2 Samuel 24:14: "Then David said to Gad, 'I am in great distress. Let us fall into the hand of the LORD, for his mercy is great; but let me not fall into the hand of man.'"

David was safe in the hands of God because of two things working together: the power of the Lord and the mercy of the Lord. If the Lord was merciful but not powerful, He would be able to comfort us but not protect us from the other forces of this world. It would be a shallow comfort, wavering in the seasons and weak against attack, disappointments, and enemies. However, if the Lord was all powerful but not merciful, His hand would also be unsafe, for apart from God's mercy, we are objects of his wrath (Eph. 2:3). His power is great, but His mercy is greater still. It triumphs over judgment (James 2:13).

And so, when we humble ourselves in surrender to God, we have assurance that He is capable. His power surrounds our little selves like the picture of the sheep in the hand of a giant. Nothing will come to us that He has not seen. He is an impenetrable security for our souls.

HIS HANDS COMFORT US

Just as we shouldn't hold back from the power of the Lord, we shouldn't hold back from the abundance of His comfort, either. Yes, His hands are mighty, but they are hands that *care for us.*

Back to 1 Peter 5:6–7: "Humble yourselves, therefore, under the mighty hand of God so that at the proper time he may exalt you, casting all your anxieties on him, because he cares for you."

I've never been much for throwing things (except parties), so the illustration of throwing our worries to God can be a bit lost on me. After all, when I throw, things don't go very far. What if I fail the throw? What does it mean to cast our anxieties on God? Is it like pitching a baseball? What if I never do it right?

We can't forget that Peter was a fisherman by trade. *Cast* isn't just a synonym for *throw*. He is alluding to casting a fishing net. A casting net is a wide, circular net that fishermen use to catch small fish. To cast it, the fisherman must throw it in the air to spread its circumference before it hits the water. A line is connected to the net, which allows the fisherman to keep hold of the net and drag it aboard when full. We see this exact kind of fishing in action in John 21. If you're as confused as I was about how casting nets look, just YouTube it.

However, in the case of 1 Peter 5, we cast without keeping the end of the net in our hands. When we cast our anxieties on the Lord, we release the net into the ocean. We spread out our worries, the grand sum of them, and watch them hit the water in full circumference. We let go of the net. We watch it sink down, down, down. Therefore, we don't have to throw it far or hard for it to be impossibly out of reach, lost within the millions of tons of water that is an ocean. It's not that our ability to cast our cares on Him eliminates our worries, it's that His ability and power to care for us covers it all.

Do you have worries today? Toss them into the ocean of God's care for you. Do you have cares that weigh you down and keep you thinking about yourself? Throw off everything that hinders (Heb. 12:1). Do you clasp tight your desire for how your life should go? That, too, needs to sink into the ocean of God's care for you.

You might argue that your cares are important. If you don't worry about them, who will? If you don't hold them, catastrophe will strike. This is reality for most of us. There are heavy things in our lives and constant responsibilities. 1 Peter 5:7 isn't a call to throw off responsibility, but to first take our cares to the Lord and act in the safety of His hands.

Imagine tossing a diamond ring into the ocean. It's not because the ring is unimportant that you'll never find it again; it's because the ocean is so vast. It's not that our anxieties aren't significant or real (Peter knows about real anxieties—in fact, much of 1 Peter is about real, hard suffering). It's that the ocean of God's care for us is *more* significant and absolutely real. His care for us is so wide and deep and high and long that we'll never find those cares again. They are drowned in the ocean of His love for us.

Perhaps, after tossing the heavy, expensive worries into the vast, deep ocean of God's care for us, we will be able to move more freely in response to life. We will be better able to care for our sick families. We will be able to handle the pressure of work without having to tie our identities to it. We will function in the midst of relationship tussles because we are secure in God's care for us.

Let that sink in. God cares for you. He cares for you with fatherly affection. For some this is a comforting notion; for others, it's hard. When I say that God is our Father, though, I do not mean that He is like our earthly fathers. No, He is our *perfect* Father—what our earthly fathers fall short of. However, there are many attributes of a good earthly father that point us to God.

My dad is amazing. One year he delivered flowers to my house late on Valentine's Day just so I would know I am loved. He had to work on my birthday this year, but that didn't stop him from stopping by just to give me a hug, even after working fourteen hours. He's the first person I call when I'm in trouble. He's the one I depend on to help me with furniture moving needs, financial decisions, and dead mice situations (that's a story for a different day).

But however great my earthly dad is, my heavenly Father is better.

> If you then, who are evil, know how to give good
> gifts to your children, how much more will your
> Father who is in heaven give good things to those
> who ask him!
>
> —MATTHEW 7:11

That is a small representation of our Heavenly Father's love for us. He has hands of comfort not because we deserve it, but because that is who He is.

With outstretched arms, we hold our hands open to God, but He doesn't leave them out cold and wet. When we open our fingers around our plans and hopes and desires, He doesn't take those things away and leave us exposed. To cast our anxieties, important as they may be, isn't to accept defeat in areas of life that we care deeply about. It is a vulnerable state to have our hands open to the Lord, and He doesn't take advantage of us. No, He places what is *best* in our hands, His own. He wraps His hands around our small ones and warms them up from the cold of this world. He shelters them from those who seek to harm us. We are protected in His grasp, for He upholds us. What may seem like a sacrifice is an upgrade, and we can rejoice in the warmth, sureness, and comfort of God's love for us.

HIS HANDS GUIDE US

The awe of knowing God's mighty hand and the comfort of feeling His fatherly affection are deep treasures, but what about when life simply sucks? Is *this* God's best effort to care for us? Is this suffering and unfairness truly an expression of His authority and love? It doesn't always add up. Is He still here?

Peter doesn't leave these questions unanswered in these two verses. For not only do we see God's powerful and caring hand, but we see His perfect guidance and timing.

> Humble yourselves, therefore, under the mighty hand of God **so that at the *proper* time he may exalt you,** casting all your anxieties on him, because he cares for you.
>
> —1 PETER 5:6–7, emphasis mine

God is the keeper of the proper time. He isn't afraid of things looking grim because He knows the end and is guiding us to *that* glory. So, in between the urge to humble ourselves and the invitation to cast all of our cares on God, Peter reminds us that the timing of these endeavors is in God's hands. It is okay that we don't see things happen in the way that we want because God is still guiding and working and leading. At the proper time, He *will* exalt us.

Although God doesn't give us the play-by-play of His plan for our lives, He does give us some major spoilers.

"And after you have suffered a little while, the God of all grace, who has called you to his eternal glory in Christ, will himself restore, confirm, strengthen, and establish you" (1 Pet. 5:10).

We glimpse the ending here. It is one of restoration, confirmation, strength, and establishment. The ending is one of abundant grace and the glory of the Lord. The ending is one of no more tears and the enlightening presence of God. We may not know the path, but we know the Way. We may be surrounded by the lies of the world, but we know the Truth. We may be in a season of darkness, but we know the Light.

> If I take the wing of the morning and dwell in the uttermost parts of the sea, even there your hand shall lead me, your right hand shall hold me. If I say, "surely the darkness shall cover me, and the light around me be night," even the darkness is

not dark to you; the night is bright as the day, for darkness is as light with you.

—PSALM 139:9–12

It says here in God's Word that His hand *holds* us, even in the extremes of life and our own inabilities. It says here in God's Word that His hand shall *lead* us. His hand is a guiding one at *all* times, even if it is not in our timing.

The answer to what our hearts long for is *yes* in Christ. It may not happen when we want it or how we want it, but healing is always a yes from God, marriage is always a yes from God, restoration is always a yes from God, security is always a yes from God. However, sometimes that healing, marriage, restoration, and security happens on the other side of this earthly life. We will be healed and with our Groom, secure and made right forever. We can long for that day even as we desire these things on Earth, too.

* * *

So, friend, wherever you are now, let Him hold you. Let Him lead you. You might be in a sunny place, and if so, I rejoice with you. Do not forget the hand of the Lord. Do not lean on your own understanding. However, you might be in a place of darkness. The same applies for you. Do not forget the Lord. Do not lean on your own feelings. The darkness is as light to Him, and He will not let you go. His grasp on you is tight and tender all at the same time.

> The steps of a man are established by the LORD, when he delights in his way; though he fall, he shall not be cast headlong, for the LORD upholds his hand.
>
> —PSALM 37:23–24

GROWING ROOTS

► How can you recognize God's hand of power in circumstances of fear in your life?

► What do you need to cast into the ocean of God's care for you?

► What decision is heavy today that you can bring to God's hands of guidance?

CHAPTER NINE

The Open Hands of Christ

He Doesn't Lead Us To Where
He Hasn't Already Gone

You stroll along the path,
winding in the wilderness.
There's brush on either side,
but it's bent beneath your feet.

The brush it snares your coat,
but it doesn't cut your legs.
Look and see a Pioneer,
His hands are working hard.

He's cutting 'way the brush,
making clear the path.
You look down again and see
the blood from His good work.

You see His footprints in the dirt.
You follow where He leads.
He didn't ask for followers
where he hasn't gone before.

I saved it for bedtime. I did all of my thinking then.

It was the longest prayer ever to a five-year-old, as I laid there and gave my life to Christ. It wasn't the prayer they said at the altar call. It covered my whole life. I knew that I needed Jesus, not just in that moment but in every moment after that. Following Him meant changing everything about my life, so I took each area of my little-girl life and specifically dedicated it to the Lord.

Because I was following Jesus now, that meant obeying my parents. That meant keeping my room clean. That meant sharing Him with others. It meant that my whole life would be His and I would follow where He went.

I remember going to church that week. Everyone kept asking if I "let Jesus into my heart." Those words fell dead on the burgundy carpet for me. I felt embarrassed to answer that question, because even at five, I understood that was not how it worked.

"I'm following Jesus," I replied. I didn't ask Him into my heart, He brought me into His. I'm not asking Him to follow my heart around, I'm following His heart around.

From that moment, I knew this was a life of following. I invite you to consider that when we say that we are following Jesus, we are saying that He has already been there! When we follow Jesus by keeping our plans in open hands, it is not Him helping us along a path He didn't pave. No, we are walking in the cut underbrush flattened by His steps.

Christ is necessary if we are going to keep our plans in open hands because He not only showed us how to do this, but He is the supplier of our healing and saving, and His resurrection keeps us His forevermore.

Every Old Testament story has a gospel-sized hole in it. Job sees Christ from afar, and many of his questions cannot be answered apart from Christ. The sacrifice of Isaac makes no sense if the Cross isn't coming. It's impossible to answer questions of pain, disappointment, and sorrow apart from the story of Jesus Christ. Our surrender is only safe in the hands of the gospel, for there the will of God is perfectly displayed as for our good and His glory.

What blows my mind is that even Christ had to open his hands to the will of God so that we might safely dwell in His hands. Before we could even entertain the idea of whole-heartedly trusting God, Christ had to whole-heartedly trust God. Before we were alive to tell the tale, He made us alive by suffering the Cross.

There are several times that the Bible specifically mentions the hands of Christ, and although "open hands" is a metaphor, I think that these verses are a clear point of how the compassion, sacrifice, and sustaining power of Christ help us to believe Him. Not only that, but these verses show that Christ Himself surrendered to the will of God. He goes before us as the founder and perfecter of our faith. He doesn't call us to do something He wouldn't do. God doesn't call us to trust Him as some kind of power move. He called even Christ to trust Him into the pain, into the suffering. If trusting the Lord wasn't what was best, Christ wouldn't have chosen that path, and God wouldn't have set it before Him.

Let's walk in the footsteps of Christ's healing, saving, and sustaining.

THE OUTSTRETCHED HANDS OF HEALING

First, we see the tender nearness of Jesus's work in our lives through how He healed people: "And a leper came to him, imploring him, and kneeling said to him, 'If you will, you can make me clean.' Moved with pity, he stretched out his hand and touched him and said to him, 'I will; be clean.' And immediately the leprosy left him, and he was made clean" (Mark 1:40-42).

Jesus's ministry was one of touching. He drew near, got His hands dirty, and interacted with His people. He didn't come down from heaven and chill, aloof from the crowd, until the time of the Cross came around. Instead,

He touched the lepers, held the children, gathered the sinners, broke the bread, and lifted up the faces of the afflicted.

Lepers were, by Law, unclean. This wasn't for their shame but for the protection of the community, so we must first understand that the Law is still good. The Law reflected God's will for His people to not get sick, thus God gave the first quarantine instructions. However, Christ came to heal His people. He came not to tell us how to be better but to make us better. He came not to simply obey the Law for us but to bring us alongside Him in His plan for redemption.

I think that this leper understood the attitude of open hands more than most anyone I know. He was really suffering. He was isolated, considered religiously unclean, physically hurting, and didn't have a path forward. We think Job lost it all, but this guy might have had even less than Job.

When the leper comes to Christ, however, he doesn't beg for healing. He doesn't question God's goodness. He doesn't demand answers or hold his fists in the air lamenting this hardship. Honestly, all of these responses would have been understandable and acceptable. Many others came to Christ in this way, so why not this man?

No, instead this leper comes to Christ and believes. *If you will, you can make me clean.* This isn't a "prove your goodness by healing me" situation. This isn't a "can you heal me?" situation. This is a "your will" situation. He isn't asking for proof, but mercy. He's on his knees, his hands open before Christ, declaring to Christ and his own soul that if Christ wants to make him well, Christ can do it.

Christ is then moved by pity. The phrasing here literally says that his bowels were moved. Now, the Scripture isn't suggesting that Jesus's digestion was affected by the leper's suffering, but rather the core of His being. "The bowels were regarded as the seat of the more violent passions, such as anger and love; but by the Hebrews as the seat of the tenderer affections, esp. kindness, benevolence, compassion; hence our heart."[21] He stretches out His hand and heals the leper. He wills! His heart is for us, not against us! He delights in showing mercy!

The question that the leper asks is in contrast with the question of the father in Mark 9 that we talked about in Chapter Five. The father asked, "But if you can do anything, have compassion on us and help us" (Mark

---

21 "Lexicon: Strong's G4698: *splagchnon*," Blue Letter Bible, 2023, https://www.blueletterbible.org/lexicon/g4698/kjv/tr/0-1/.

9:22). The leper, however, states that Christ can, if He wills, make him clean. The father has his hands knuckle-white around the outcome of healing, to the point that he couldn't see Christ clearly. The leper has his hands, white with leprosy, open before the will of God. The father doubts; the leper believes. The father begs for compassion; the leper falls to his knees.

What makes my soul wonder at the mercy of Christ is that He heals *both*. He heals the open-handed leper and the son of the struggling father. He stretches out His hand with mercy to those who come before Him humbly and those who can't see straight through their pain. He doesn't restrain his mercy toward those struggling to come before Him (Ps. 40:11). Christ rebukes the father's lack of faith, but He still heals the son.

Why? Because He delights in mercy, in healing, and in hope. "Who is a God like you, pardoning iniquity and passing over transgression for the remnant of his inheritance? He does not retain his anger forever, because he delights in steadfast love." (Mic. 7:18). It is not the worthiness of the recipient or even the magnitude of faith, but it is the mercy of Christ that heals.

Christ's hands of healing pave the way for us to trust Him more with our hurt, our sickness, and our sorrow.

His mercy cuts the sharp underbrush of suffering in our lives.

THE OUTSTRETCHED HANDS OF SAVING

The most powerful illustration of Christ's hands is seen on the Cross: "Then Jesus went with them to a place called Gethsemane ... And going a little further he fell on his face and prayed, saying, 'My Father, if it be possible, let this cup pass from me; nevertheless, not as I will, but as you will'" (Matt. 26:36, 39).

> Now from the sixth hour there was darkness over all the land until the ninth hour. And about the ninth hour Jesus cried out with a loud voice, saying "Eli, Eli lema sabachthani?" that is, "My God, my God, why have you forsaken me?" And some of the bystanders, hearing it, said, "This man is calling Elijah." And one of them at once ran and took a sponge, filled it with sour wine, and put it on a reed and gave it to him to drink. But the others said, "Wait, let us see whether Elijah will come to save him." And Jesus cried out again with a loud voice and yielded up his spirit.
>
> —MATTHEW 27:45-50

Consider this moment, my friends. Consider your Savior, His desires open in His hands as He surrenders to the suffering of not only the pain of the Cross but the separation from God that sin creates. Consider the sweat drops of blood that dripped from His forehead onto His outstretched hands to heaven. Here in this moment of prayer before the Cross, He could have thrown in the towel and walked away. He had every right.

Consider the agony of the Cross as His hands stretched out wide. "For the joy that was set before him endured the cross, despising the shame" (Heb. 12:2). But it was shameful. Crowds gathered to shame him. The soldiers gambled over his clothes. Even the sun hid its face. Consider the outstretched hands of Christ.

Because Christ faced the forsaken moment of the Cross, God will never forsake us.

Let that sink in.

The Cross is a dark place. We can picture the physical pain and the weight of sin but imagine the emotional depth of pain that the forsaken moment of the Cross held. Christ had never experienced this kind of separation from God's perfect communion and delight. His anchor was much more firmly in God's love and commitment than ours is. He hadn't known a moment, a millisecond, without God's full support and peace.

I've been following Jesus for almost twenty years now, so I have a unique and cherished life that has treasured the constant love of God for almost as long as I can remember. At every turn, He has been there. He's been faithful again and again. His steadfastness roots my life in so many ways. I don't know what it is to not stand upon Him. I don't want to know that. He is my treasured companion and *the* way that I process life.

Christ, however, experienced an eternity of perfect unity and support. Not twenty years. Eternity. Yet He gave that up. He faced the darkness of our sin and the punishment of our rebellion. He endured the Cross for the *joy* of doing the will of the Father, that we might be able to enter into a covenant of steadfast love, that we may be able to stand upon the grace of God and face tomorrow.

What depth of love.

What then shall we say to these things? If our God is for us, who can be against us? He who did not spare his own Son but gave him up for us all, how will he not also with him graciously give us all things? . . . For I am sure that neither death nor life, nor angels nor rules, nor things present nor things to come, nor powers, nor height nor depth, nor anything else in all creation, will be able to separate us from the love of God in Christ Jesus our Lord.

—ROMANS 8:31–32, 38–39

That is our sure confidence in God's un-forsaking love. Christ considered it worthwhile to endure the darkness of the Cross so that we may know and cherish the steadfast love of the Lord as He does. Christ stretched out His hands on the cross that we might be held in the favor of God's will.

But God did not abandon Him to Sheol. Death could not hold Him. Sin was not too much for Him. The depth of every person's sin didn't weigh Him down for long. Three days later, *He rose from the grave.*

We know that Christ, being raised from the dead, will never die again; death no longer has dominion over him. For the death he died he died to sin, once for all, but the life he lives, he lives to God. So you also must consider you yourselves dead to sin and alive to God in Christ Jesus.

—ROMANS 6:9–11

Christ did face the moment of forsakenness on the Cross, but He has won an eternity of life, salvation, and redemption.

Consequently, He is always able to save to the uttermost those we draw near to God through him, since he always lives to make intercession for them.

—HEBREWS 7:25

This is our confidence. He will always live to intercede for us, to keep our feet from slipping, to provide grace upon grace, and to be our perfection. He is our Advocate, and He will never die, leave that position, or be forced out. It is a done deal, Christ and His church. It is a marriage never to be annulled. It is a covenant never to be broken.

This is the rock on which we stand. This is our confidence. When we open our hands around our plans, we can have confidence in the Lord's heart towards us because of the open hands of Christ upon the Cross. As pointed out in Chapter Three, we can have confidence in the goodness of God for our hearts because *the Cross says so.* When it is difficult to keep our plans in open hands, we can take courage from the Cross as we follow in Christ's ways.

THE OUTSTRETCHED HANDS OF KEEPING

Jesus didn't stop there. His hands have scars to forever remind us of His power over sin and His mercy to us: "Then he said to Thomas, 'Put your finger here, and see my hands; and put out your hand, and place it in my side. Do not disbelieve, but believe'" (John 20:27).

Oh, how we throw shade at Thomas, but this entire book is about the very struggle that Thomas had. Thomas struggled to trust the Lord. He struggled to open up his hands around what he considered true. He feared the utter disappointment of losing Christ again. The others saw Christ—they had the evidence and felt the joy—but I feel Thomas's reluctance. It seemed too good to be true. Sometimes trusting the Lord feels like we're believing something too good. How could Jesus really be alive? Does this really change everything?

What does Christ do when He sees Thomas? He opens up His hands.

Read that again.

Christ doesn't strike Thomas for his unbelief even as He didn't ridicule Peter on the water. Instead, He opens his hands and invites Thomas to believe. Thomas wanted proof; here's proof. Thomas needed a sign before trusting; here's a sign. Look at Christ's hands. Though He was in a perfected, resurrected body and God could have chosen to heal those wounds, He left them. There were still marks from the grueling hours on the cross, perhaps scabbed over and very unlikely the clean little holes that we see in Sunday School pictures. Why would God leave those marks in Christ's hands if not to encourage us all, perhaps most specifically Thomas, that it really is *true?* Christ really did rise from the grave, and His hands are outstretched for us to *believe.*

Christ invites Thomas to examine His hands. He takes the clenched fists of Thomas and invites Thomas to instead grasp His own hands. He convicts Thomas of his disbelief yet specifically provides for what Thomas desires. He shows Thomas that what Thomas wanted wasn't to see the proof. What Thomas wanted was assurance. Assurance that it was all real. Assurance that the Cross didn't have the final say. Assurance that the grave was empty. As it turns out, the presence of Christ alone was enough. Thomas would have believed even without the nail marks, but Christ gave that to Thomas anyway.

What I find particularly striking about this is that it shows that Jesus lives so that He may *continue* to strengthen our faith. He is now forever making intercession for us, that we may not clench our hands around that which kills but that which gives life. He forever lives that we may see and taste His deep love for us and trust Him. He forever lives that we may be more and more believing, and thus more and more Christlike.

Christ is not afraid of our disbelief. He doesn't shudder at our inability to trust. He doesn't give up on our clenched fists. Instead, Christ opens His hands to us that we may believe, and not just believe but *be sustained* in belief. Because Christ never will die again, we have a confidence that we can continually have our plans in open hands because Christ is continually alongside us. He carries on His work in us until completion (Phil. 1:6).

* * *

The gospel isn't a figure-it-out-and-then-go kind of message. It is a watch-then-copy lifestyle. We get to see, through the Word, Christ surrender to God's will time and time again. He let go of cultural norms. He opened His hands, letting go of what was comfortable and easy. He surrendered to the point of death so that we could be kept forever in His healing, saving, sustaining grasp. We have a great leader who understands and overcomes every obstacle in the way of us trusting God.

GROWING ROOTS

► How does Christ's example encourage you to surrender?
► Do you relate more to the leper or Thomas?
► What is one act of obedience that you can do to follow Christ today?

Now Go

*Changing the narrative of our minds
to trust the Lord even when it's hard*

CHAPTER TEN

Waiting Trust

Open Hands Worship in the Waiting

It's not loud, but it distorts every song.
It's not heavy, but it weighs you down.
It's not sharp, but it saws at your heart.
It's not big, but it takes too much space.
It's waiting.
And we need to learn to let it be
loud, heavy, sharp, and big.

I have curly, thin, brown hair. It's a big part of my personality, and I love that God curls my hair for me every morning. Thus, I let it do its thing. I'm so low-maintenance that if a hairstyle isn't finished in two red lights, it takes too long. Gradually, I have added blonde to my hair, though, and the past couple of times I colored my hair, its texture changed. My hair has become drier and tangles *so* easily. Now, instead of a quick brush after the shower and *voila*, I spend at least five minutes getting the rat's nest out of my hair.

It brings me back to seven-year-old Hannah. When I was seven, after playing outside for hours, my curly hair and little bangs became a rat's nest that made me resemble a poodle more than a little girl. (I have to constantly remind myself of those days when I'm tempted to get bangs again.) If I'm low-maintenance about my hair now, I was even lower-maintenance as a child. I would take the brush and yank the knots out of my hair, unworried about the casualties. Sure, it hurt a little bit, but it was efficient.

However, when my daddy brushed my hair, he carefully took one strand at a time and removed it from the tangle. Slowly, methodically, the knotted mess would disappear, and not a hair would be torn. He wasn't in a rush. He knew how delicate my hair was and that to move too quickly would ruin it. When I would chide him for taking too long, he would remind me that my hair was important. It was worth the slow untangle.

I think about that every time I brush my hair now. I think about how my daddy patiently detangled my hair as a child. When I am tempted to rush through the process, unfazed by the breakage, I slow down and remember that it is worth the wait.

Just so, perhaps in the times of life when we are waiting, the Lord is carefully untangling. We want to rush ahead to the next step, regardless of the breakage, but He cares about every strand, every step. He knows how many strands of hair are on our head and wills that we don't lose more than needed. He is taking His time, tenderly brushing through our lives in these periods of waiting. It is never wasted and always worth it.

In some way or another, we are all waiting for something. Some of us are in obvious times of waiting in our lives. We wait for illness to go away, loved ones to be saved, or a promotion at our jobs. We wait to get married, to be able to have children, or to be able to move. However, there are smaller areas of waiting, too. Maybe you are waiting for enough money in the bank account to be able to buy your first home. Perhaps you want to move into a bigger home so not all four of your children are sharing a bathroom. It could be waiting to dwell in community when your world feels lonely. Maybe you're waiting to understand the next step in your career, or for the culture to reflect the kingdom. Maybe it seems daunting. Sometimes we wait for simple things like Christmas or for our hair to grow back after that terrible choice to get bangs.

Waiting is a normal and frequent period of our lives, but it is hard. It is a heavy thing, this waiting. Unlike suffering, waiting is a dull pain, but a pain nonetheless. It is like a weighted blanket. If a fifteen-pound dumbbell fell on someone's chest, it would crush them. People would come running to see if they were okay. However, if a fifteen-pound weighted blanket was spread over someone, no one would notice. Just because the pain is spread out over a multitude of days doesn't make it less heavy.

Our waiting hearts tend to look for outcomes, answers, and feelings, but of the three, I think that waiting mostly wants an answer. Let's take singleness, for example. I'm currently single, and one of the deepest desires of my heart is to be married. As I get older, this desire becomes stronger, and the distance between where I am and where I want to be, and where my friends are, becomes greater. However, I have a lot on my plate and love the life that God has given me today. The struggle is not that today is too hard to bear; the struggle is the fear that tomorrow may be too hard. If I only *knew* that in four years I'd be married, I would live these four years fiercely at work in singleness, confident in the Lord's provision over the desires of my heart. Alternatively, if I knew I was never getting married, I would adjust my hopes now and live accordingly.

But I don't know if I will be married in four years, four months, or ever. I don't hold that answer. Thus, I must live today fiercely at work in singleness despite *not* having the answer of when or if I will get married. The rough part of this kind of waiting is that sometimes we are not told to forgo the dream or the work. We are called, rather, to still dream it and wait. Should I, in an attempt to protect my heart, give up on the idea of marriage for fear that I'll get my hopes up for nothing? Not at all. I am called to hope, dream, and plan with open hands in the waiting. That is hard. Should you, in an attempt to forgo the pain of disappointment, abandon your dream of planting a church, growing your family, or moving into a different home? Not at all. Sometimes we are just called to hold those dreams in open hands and *wait*.

There are a lot of *true* things about waiting that I see on Instagram or that people tell me. I find, however, that they aren't *helpful* for the person waiting. "Your time will come." "There's a purpose for the waiting." "This is just preparing you." "It'll all work out." "God has a plan."

These things may all very well be true, but as someone accustomed to the waiting season, I don't find them to be particularly helpful. They sound shallow. They sound like they're trying to make me feel better by sugar-coating the truth. They're all outcome-, feeling-, and answer-based comforts, and we've already debunked that these kinds of answers are fickle.

Perhaps the best solace in the waiting is some very un-sugar-coated truth. Perhaps what our waiting souls need to do is praise the Lord.

Waiting isn't always a situation to be changed, a feeling to erase, or a problem to be answered. Sometimes it is simply that—waiting. Perhaps an open-handed approach to the areas in life where we find ourselves waiting isn't to understand more but to sit more. Perhaps it's not to have the next step figured out but to look around at where you are now. Perhaps it's not to yank the knot out but to let our Father carefully untangle it. Perhaps it isn't to rid ourselves of the hurt of waiting but bring that hurt to Christ.

If waiting is a big trend of our lives, then it seems natural to see that it isn't bad; rather, it is meant to point us to Christ. Waiting isn't the Lord taking His time; it is the Lord's time to grow our hearts. Waiting isn't an empty season of preparation; it is *life*. We don't have to wait for marriage, kids, the promotion, or the vacation to start living fully for the Lord. That is for *now*. That is for *here*. I think you already know that, though. The trouble is that we can't just *know* that our lives are meant for now. We have to *live* like it.

If I were to pick one person who tells our hearts how to wait, it would be my namesake, Hannah.

Hannah desires a child. She longs for a child. She is made for bringing a child into the world. She looks around and doesn't have to look far to see others getting her desire. Peninnah, Hannah's husband's other wife (does that make her a wife-in-law?), didn't waste any chance to rub salt in the wound for Hannah. We don't know much about Peninnah except that she had many children and that she bullied Hannah. I can't help but think that Hannah must have felt that, of the two of them, Peninnah deserved to be barren more than she did. Hannah's spiritual depth reveals that she pursued the Lord for some time. For Hannah to see every day how Peninnah's careless life was so blessed must have hurt. I feel that.

We do that, too. *Why does she get that nice car when she drives it so recklessly? I work so hard and drive a dump. Why does she get to be married and happy when I know she was careless with her heart and intentions? I have prayed and fought for this time and time again, and life has left me heartbroken. Why? Why?*

God has a far more glorious plan for us than what is fair. He has grace in store for us, and that is the opposite of fair. Grace is getting what we do not deserve, so when we start to question the fairness of things, remember that Jesus's grace given to us is the most unfair thing we've ever experienced.

Hannah means *grace*. I've always loved that. In the middle of a long season of waiting, God is about to bestow great grace upon Hannah, but more importantly, to His entire nation—and us, also. What happened to Hannah wasn't fair; it was grace. That is far more abundant than fair.

There is much to learn from the life of Hannah and Samuel, but I want to glean three things with you in relation to how Hannah waited.

HANNAH DIDN'T SHY FROM THE PAIN OF WAITING

The Scripture says that Hannah wept (1 Sam. 1:7). It says that she was "deeply distressed and prayed to the Lord and wept bitterly" (1 Sam. 1:9). She didn't hide from the sadness. She didn't mask the sorrow—not from her adversaries, her husband, or, most notably, the Lord. She was sad, and it sounds like she was a bit dramatic about it.

Waiting can be sad. This is the un-sugar-coated truth. Waiting can be a bitter time, a sad time, a crying time. Hannah doesn't, in her sadness, ignore or blame the Lord. She instead brings it to him. She draws near. She brings all her disappointment, bitterness, sorrow, and hopes to the Lord in prayer and weeps bitterly. She comes to the Lord in her deep vexation and anxiety (1 Sam. 1:16).

Oh, have I been there.

Sometimes, when the sorrow of waiting gets too much I like to find a quiet spot and cry it out. I name each thing that weighs heavy, and I ask the Lord this question: "Can you handle my hurt?"

"Can you handle the hurt of a broken heart?" I ponder this question, remembering who God is. *Yes,* I say to my heart. *Yes, He can handle my broken heart.*

Then I go onto the next thing heavy on my heart.

"I know you can handle my broken heart, but what about my fears about failing? Can you handle that, too?"

Yes, He can handle that, too.

Then I specifically bring each of my sorrows and cares before the Lord and acknowledge that He can handle all of them. He can handle all of our sorrow. Follow Hannah's lead as she "pours out [her] soul" (1 Sam. 1:15).

One of my dear friends, in her season of waiting, told me that she needs to get comfortable sitting in it. She doesn't rush around to try and fix it. She doesn't ignore it. She gets to know the season of waiting for what it is. She looks for ways she can know the Lord better in the disappointments. I have seen this friend time and time again face the things-not-yet with gentle courage that comes from someone who is comfortable with it.

Don't be afraid of the waiting. Don't be afraid to sit and face your sorrow. Don't be afraid of its depth, for the Lord is mightier. To see the chasm of pain is only to make God greater for crossing that chasm. He isn't afraid of your broken heart, either.

In this acknowledgement of the hard, there is courage. If we ready our hearts for the hard, it isn't so bad. There is our answer. We roll up our sleeves and say to our hearts, "This is hard, but hard isn't bad. Once I stop being afraid of the hard, the real work can begin." Sometimes that real work, though, looks more like sitting than running.

Specifically name those burdens and ask the Lord if He can handle them. Keep asking Him until you can think of nothing else, and at the end of your lists of sorrow you will find that He *can* handle them all. He can hold them all as you present them with open hands.

HANNAH DIDN'T SHY FROM
THE HOPE OF WAITING

Hope hurts. If we didn't hope for anything, we wouldn't get our hopes dashed. If we didn't love anything, we wouldn't get our hearts broken. If we didn't dream anything, we wouldn't have our dreams disappointed. It is an act of courage to hope and not give into despondency or pessimism.

How many years did Hannah enter the house of the Lord and ask for a child? Many. The Scripture says, "so it went on year after year" (1 Sam. 1:7). How many times did Hannah cry out to the Lord for His provision? More than she could count, I'm sure. Yet, she didn't give up hope. How do I know? Because she *kept asking*.

Even in her vexation and anxiety, she showed up and kept asking. She feared that God had forgotten her, but she hoped that He hadn't. She feared that the Lord wouldn't give her a child, but she hoped that He would. She hoped that what she knew of God was true. Allistar Begg, in his sermon on 1 Samuel, said, "God's love in the past is what gives her the confidence to pray as audaciously as she does."[22]

Elizabeth Elliot said, "So when the answer was no with the thorn in the flesh, and for Jesus' prayer in Gethsemane, we know there's nothing wrong with praying that God will solve our problems and heal our diseases and pay our debts and sort out our marital difficulties. It's right and proper that we should bring our requests to God. We're not praying against His will.

---

22 Alistair Begg, "Only Her Lips Moved," February 6, 2019, YouTube, 37:20, https://www.youtube.com/watch?v=wV0l-mODGbs.

But when the answer is no, then we know that God has something better at stake. There is another level, another kingdom, an invisible kingdom which you and I cannot see now but toward which we move and to which we belong."[23]

Here we see the connection of suffering, perseverance, character, and hope as detailed in Romans 5:3–5: "More than that, we rejoice in our sufferings, knowing that suffering produces endurance, and endurance produces character, and character produces hope, and hope does not put us to shame, because God's love has been poured into our hearts through the Holy Spirit who has been given to us."

Hannah's suffering (the waiting for a child) made her endure and bend her knee to the Lord. This perseverance created character in Hannah so that she knew that the Lord was mighty and worthy and able to do all things. Then she hoped in who she thought God to be. Hannah thought God to be a god who looks upon the afflicted, thus she hoped that He would attend to her hurt. That hope did not put her to shame.

I, too, know the struggle of hope. However, I chose not to hope and disguised it as holiness.

---

23 Lisa Appelo, "50 Elizabeth Elliott Quotes on Suffering," Lisa Appelo, May 28, 2021, https://lisaappelo.com/ elisabeth-elliot-quotes-on-suffering/.

People often say to me, "When you get married…" For the longest time, I would correct them. "If it be God's will I get married," I would say. I felt as if this was helping me keep my plans in open hands. After all, nothing is guaranteed to us apart from the spiritual blessings of the gospel. The scripture doesn't say that all who want to get married will get married. There *is* an "if" there. I don't think it wise to assume that our lives will go the way culture, our families, or even the church sometimes expects them to go.

However, I didn't say "if it be God's will that I get married" because I was so submissive to God's plan. It wasn't a holier-than-thou situation; it was rooted in fear that He wouldn't be good. *Don't get your hopes up, Hannah, because God might hold out on you on this one. Best not even to hope. Perhaps His will isn't all good and perfect.*

I've since been convicted of that pride. You will laugh at what has shown me this lesson most clearly: the movie *Tangled*. It's my favorite movie of all time and forever, somewhat because I'm a huge Disney fan and love princesses, but mostly because of this lesson that God taught me through this movie.

In *Tangled*, Rapunzel longed to see the floating lights. Year after year she would watch from the window as the lights passed by on her birthday. It was her dream. Along the adventure to realizing her dream, she meets Eugene, the rough-on-the-outside-sweet-within dreamboat. He brings her to see the lanterns and in one magical moment, she gets what she dreamed of, only to realize that her old dream didn't matter so much anymore. The man next to her captivated her more than the lanterns, and Rapunzel realizes that he is her new dream.

I venture to say that the movie could have been lovely if Rapunzel had never seen the lanterns. Sure, we would have missed out on the most beautiful scene in any Disney movie, but Rapunzel would have been okay if some other adventure had happened, she didn't see the lanterns, and instead she just fell in love with Eugene. But that's not how the story goes. She got both.

I think my dream of getting married is like Rapunzel's dream of seeing the lanterns. It's something that I long for and work to make happen. Along the way, though, I find that my new and better dream is not the lanterns. It's not marriage, a career, or personal fulfillment. It is the One who is with me. It is the Lord. He has captivated me, and even if I never get those other dreams, it is a good story.

But that's not always how the story goes. Sometimes we get both. To say "take the world and give me Jesus," does not *necessarily mean* that you won't get anything that you want here on Earth. Some of those dreams in your heart are of the Lord. Some of the things that you long to accomplish are how He is going to work for you. Sometimes we need to press on in hope toward the secondary dreams, assured and strengthened that our primary dream is already fulfilled. He longs to be gracious to us (Isa. 30:18). He may be far more abundant to us than all we ask or imagine (Eph. 3:20).

It's not that I assume that I'll get married; God may deem that singleness is most good and glorious. It's that I no longer expect the worst from Him. I know that His plans are good because He is good. The outcome will mirror that. So, in that assurance, I've gotten my hopes up a bit. I'm clear with my desires to the Lord and to others. It was a little silly to try and pretend otherwise.

Hannah teaches us to live a dangerously hopeful life, even when the world might tell us to move on and when our hearts get weary from the hope. Sometimes the Lord is clear to us that we are to move on to different dreams, but often in the waiting, we are called to continue to show up and ask with hope. Do not be afraid to ask with hope—not necessarily hope that we get all that we want, but assurance that the Lord will be good to us.

Just as we named all of our hurts to the Lord, let us also name all of our hopes to the Lord and let Him share in those with us. It's time to get hopeful.

HANNAH DIDN'T SHY FROM THE WORSHIP OF WAITING

Hannah's most obvious and beautiful prayer of worship is in 1 Samuel 2, but this happens *after* Samuel is born. Before Samuel is even promised, though, Hannah worships the Lord. She worships in the waiting, in the sitting, and in the hoping.

How does she worship? She surrenders her plans to the Lord's. She declares that if the Lord gives her a child, the child shall be the Lord's. She doesn't just mean in an all-I-have-is-Yours kind of way but a Nazarite-vow, I'm-going-to-drop-my-child-at-the-temple kind of way. A huge component of worship in the Israelite culture was sacrifice, something perhaps lost on us. Thus, this sacrifice of her dreams, this promise, was worship.

We don't have to wait for answers in order to praise the Lord for them. We don't have to wait for the outcome to praise the Lord for His salvation. As I said before, the waiting is *life*. We are called to worship while we wait.

This is *the* un-sugar-coated truth that we need to repeat to our souls in times of waiting. We don't need to repeat, "It'll all work out." We don't need to cling to the hope of our dreams in the way we want them. We need to praise the Lord who has *already* worked it all out. We need to praise the Lord, who is the fulfillment of our heart's desires. We get to worship the Lord *while* we hope.

In the waiting, when nothing comforts and answers seem miles away, cling to the truth—the un-sugar-coated truth of who God is and what He has already done for us. The Cross has the final word, and it is *teleō*, which means "it is finished."[24] We don't need to sugar-coat that kind of truth. It is already honey to our souls and sweetness to our days, even the days of waiting.

* * *

If your hands are getting tired of waiting for someone to hold them, something to fill them, or something for them to do, remember these three pathways. When doubts come or the waiting seems hard to bear, pre-decide to turn your mind to these practices.

Name your sorrows to the Lord and ask if He can handle them (spoiler alert—He can).

---

24 Lexicon: Strong's G5055: *teleō*," Blue Letter Bible, 2023, https://www.blueletterbible.org/lexicon/g5055/esv/mgnt/0-1/.

Name your hopes before the Lord and boldly ask for them.

Worship the Lord from the finished work of the gospel, even if your life feels like a house in the middle of a renovation.

With these three habits, I hope that you and I wait in a way that honors the Lord more. Perhaps we may see that waiting isn't something to dread but something to learn from,

There is a P.S. to this chapter, though.

P.S. Hannah did bear a son. Not just that, she bore three sons and three daughters. The Lord was abundantly kind to her. He *didn't* waste her waiting. He *didn't* withhold her desires forever. He blessed her with many children and her heart, in this provision, continued to worship the Lord and give thanks.

I say this as a P.S. because I don't want us to think that by following the steps of Hannah we will get what we want. This isn't a three-step process to accomplishing our dreams. In fact, Hannah saw this clearly.

> He will guard the faithful ones, but the wicked shall be cut off in darkness, for not by might shall man prevail.
>
> —1 SAMUEL 2:9

She bore children not because of her own desires, her worthiness, or even her ability to pray. She bore children because of the Lord's faithfulness. It wasn't her might but her humility. It wasn't her forcing God's hand but opening her hand. She bore Samuel because that was the Lord's plan to lead Israel. She bore Samuel because he would choose David, who would in turn be a prequel to Jesus. Ultimately, she bore a son because it paved the way for the gospel. The point of the story is not that Hannah got what she wanted; the point of the story is the gospel. Just like any story in Scripture, really.

"She could never have known that in answering her prayer, God was actually addressing the problem of Israel. God, in answering her little prayer was doing something that was vast in its ramifications . . . when she asks the question, 'Why is this happening to me?,' the answer to that question is not in the 'this' and it's not in the 'me.' For the ways of God are vast beyond our ability to comprehend . . ."[25]

So, as we learn from Hannah, I am encouraged by the Lord's graciousness to her. I am encouraged to continue to face my waiting, ask in hope, and worship in the midst. I am encouraged that the Lord doesn't withhold children

---

25 Alistair Begg, "Only Her Lips Moved," February 6, 2019, YouTube, 37:20, https://www.youtube.com/watch?v=wV0l-mODGbs.

from Hannah just because He could. I am encouraged that our lives, in the good and the hard, point to the very best thing, the gospel.

GROWING ROOTS

▶ What weighs you down in the waiting today? Name it specifically before the Lord.

▶ What are you hoping for today?

▶ How can you change the narrative of impatience into worship?

CHAPTER ELEVEN

Habitual Trust

Daily Choices of Trust

Lists made on the back of a receipt,
scattered thoughts at a red light,
whispers of a changed mind—
these are all tiny changes,
daily habits,
small moments of life
where we think we are alone,
where we should be able to handle it,
where we don't consider that even here,
we are invited to yet bring it all to the Lord
in trust.

"Do you trust the Lord with your stretch marks?" I saw this question on Instagram, and it made me ponder. Do I trust the Lord with something as small and seemingly insignificant as a stretch mark? Do I trust the Lord with the things that I feel the responsibility to control?

I have a long history of problematic thoughts about my body, and by the grace of God, He has rescued me from many destructive behaviors and thoughts. After I broke my foot the second time, I "retired" from ballet and started channeling my energy into the gym. My discipline from ballet naturally translated into the gym until I became what some people may call a "gym rat." The results were bigger muscles and due to a more relaxed diet, a little more cushion. These changes happened rather quickly, and a few months in I noticed some stretch marks on my legs.

"That wasn't there last I looked," I thought to myself, and I began to panic. I thought about how to control my eating or reduce my gym time. Maybe there was an ointment that would rid my legs of these flaws. I started to spiral until I remembered that I could trust God with that stretch mark. Even that one. Even though I didn't like it. Even though I could take measures to get rid of it or prevent more, I also had the freedom to trust God with that little line and live my life with my eyes set on the bigger picture.

So, I get to move forward in trust with 1,000 tiny decisions going forward. I get to trust God with the habitual choice to eat when I was tempted to forgo a meal. I get to enjoy how He made me when I look in the mirror instead of nitpicking my appearance. I get to walk in trust with every tiny decision on the path to healing.

There are thousands of tiny things that we get to trust the Lord with each day.

What about trusting the Lord when Google Maps says it'll take fifteen minutes to get to your destination but you're two minutes behind, so you speed to make up the difference? Do you trust the Lord when gas prices go up again? Do you trust the Lord when your turn to do the dishes comes up more often than your roommate or spouse's? Do you trust the Lord when you text that friend first but you would prefer them to text you first?

I find that trusting the Lord is often reserved for big things like changing careers or having a child. *That's* when we need to exercise our trust. We miss so many small opportunities to trust the Lord throughout our days. Why do we do that? Shouldn't it be *easier* to trust the Lord with the little things? Why is it that, more often than not, it is the little things that we struggle with? I think this is because we think we can and *should* handle the little worries of our day. When the boss man tells us he needs the project done a day sooner than we expected, we think we should be able to roll up our sleeves and do it. When our church has a big event during a season of our lives when we're already stretched thin, we think we just have to grit our teeth and do it. When we are struggling with our daily choices to pursue health, we think that it is beneath the Lord's attention.

We approach daily life and struggles with a Nike attitude, our hands full of little worries like a twenty-something girl carrying her keys, phone, water bottle, coffee, Target bag, and chapstick at once, all hanging off of different fingers. (Yes, this is me. I'm too stubborn to get a bag.) We've got this. We can handle it.

Whereas waiting trust is releasing answers and suffering trust is releasing outcomes, habitual trust is about releasing feelings. We must let go of the feeling that we can control our lives. We cannot manifest our days, even in small ways. We get to practice trust even when we don't feel like it, and we often don't. Additionally, we get to start that practice *today*, with our car door that won't open and our in-laws who are coming to town unexpectedly.

I find myself thinking about Mary and Martha daily, because their lives point to Christ in the daily struggles and the catastrophic days of need. I teeter-totter between relating to Mary and Martha, but most of the time I'm a Martha. Let's read their story.

"Now as they went on their way, Jesus entered a village. And a woman named Martha welcomed him into her house. And she had a sister called Mary, who sat at the Lord's feet and listened to his teaching. But Martha was distracted with much serving. And she went up to him and said, 'Lord, do you not care that my sister has left me to serve alone? Tell her then to help me.' But the Lord answered her, 'Martha, Martha, you are anxious and troubled about many things, but one thing is necessary. Mary has chosen the good portion, which will not be taken away from her'" (Luke 10:38-42).

WORRIED ABOUT MANY THINGS

Martha had her hands full, literally. She was holding the bread bowl and the broom and the butter dish all on one arm. The servant came up to her and asked what to do with the calf they just slaughtered. She forgot to fix that table last week, and now people were already using it. She *should* be able to handle a guest coming over, right? This was normal. This was her job. She wanted to show the Teacher her respect, for He deserved it. The Teacher certainly didn't care about her little worries. Why wouldn't Mary just help her?

First of all, there are many things that Martha is doing right. She is hospitable, serving, and attentive to others' needs. She is doing the work, and that is more than most people can say. We tend to downplay Martha's response, but it is mostly right.

Her hands are *doing* good things, like the hands of the Proverbs 31 woman: "She opens her hands to the poor and reaches out her hands to the needy" (Prov. 31:20).

But her heart is *avoiding* the best thing.

Along the way, Martha got something mixed up. She worked so hard to get the attention of Christ's care for her when it was available all along. She didn't need to impress Christ with her service in order for Him to care about her. She didn't need to have a fresh bread basket and full water pitcher on the table in order to sit down and enjoy the Bread of Life and the Living Water. They were available to her despite the condition of the kitchen floor.

Martha feels lonely in her constant work of trying. This is often where we are at with our struggles of habitual trust. It's the little things, hanging off of each finger, that occupy our hands so that they are no longer open to the Lord. Our sense of self becomes elevated as we compare our work to the work of others. Truly, this is prideful. Along with this pride, we feel lonely, because we don't really want to be better than the rest. We want *rest*. We want care. We want to be seen. We get so distracted by trying to earn God's rest that we forget it is already there in full.

In answering Martha's plea to care for her, Christ replies, in a sense, "I care deeply for you. In fact, I care enough to show you a better way. Humble your high ambitions for a moment and let me show you how much I care."

Martha, Martha. He says this twice to be gentle. It softens the correction and invites Martha to grow instead of bristle. He invites her to pause.

You are anxious and troubled about many things. This. This is why I think Luke 10 is necessary when talking about habitual trust. Jesus isn't talking about being worried about one big thing but rather a dozen assorted things of different magnitudes. He is talking about the laundry and the family dynamics and the ministry. He is talking about the hundred tabs open in her brain. He is simply talking about life. He invites her to put her things down.

He is inviting you to put them down, too.

THE ONE THING

But one thing is necessary. This sounds beautifully simple. One thing is necessary, Christ. The only thing on the list is Christ. However, do the other needs go away? Does Martha's need to be seen and appreciated go away? Does the need to make dinner go away? Does the need to serve others go away? Does Christ's need to eat go away? No. Those are still very real, but Christ is saying that those very real needs are all *met in Him.*

The worry Martha held about what people thought of her hosting and serving is fully met by the Lord's gracious thoughts toward her. The worry that the day doesn't have enough hours is fully met by the Lord who has made time for *Martha*. The worry that Martha works alone is fully met in Christ, who invites Martha to instead work alongside Him. Christ is the specific and exact fulfillment of all of Martha's needs. As we said before, God created us with these specific longings in our hearts, and they are not bad. They are often tainted by sin, but the Lord seeks to fulfill them in Himself. After all, He made us for Himself.

As I mentioned briefly, I've struggled with how I look. Although I didn't recognize it at the time, I had an eating disorder in high school that has been a quiet overlay to my thinking for the better part of my life. The turning point for me was a moment in my senior year of high school. I was doing my shower deep-thinking (which at that time included obsessively analyzing everything I ate that day and counting the calories in my head). Piercing through my thoughts was a clear image in my brain. It was a picture of a detailed and wonderful work of art in an elaborate gold frame. Then I saw myself with a

Rose Art crayon "fixing" it. I didn't even have the name brand. With every worry and decision of distrust, I cluttered the masterpiece that never needed fixing. My actions couldn't contribute to God's work; they could only distract from it.

Do not think that the masterpiece was a perfect body. No, God's masterpiece in me was *Christ*. And my struggle in prioritizing my appearance over Christ clouded my vision of both Christ and myself. The point of releasing my insecure thoughts about my body isn't that I got to better rejoice in my own body (which I do get to do). No, the point of me releasing my worries about my body is that I can better see the One Thing that is necessary.

That One Thing is always Christ.

The object for you, too, in releasing small feelings and fears is not that those situations might be "cured." It is not so that you might feel better about yourself. No, it is so that you may see Christ more clearly. He meets the needs that we worry so much about.

Let's think practically here for a minute (I'm sure Martha would appreciate that). Christ could have stopped Martha, told her not to worry, and instantly made dinner like He did with the 5,000. He made food miraculously appear before, so why didn't He for Martha? He could have physically met her needs right then and there. Christ could miraculously make our bodies whole or the dishes clean or the bank account full. What a show of care that would be! What is He teaching Martha, and therefore us, by making her sit in the incomplete work?

WE GET TO CHOOSE

The answers to these questions are in Luke 10:42: *Mary has chosen the good portion.* Christ wants Martha to *choose.* He is teaching her soul to choose rest when busy is right there. He is teaching her heart to choose truth when the lies are right there. He is teaching her to choose Himself when the desire to choose self is right there. He doesn't take away the busy, the fear, or the desires. No, He asks for Martha's trust in these small things that pile up.

This is the start of the holy habit of trust. Even now in your life, you are probably anxious about something. Trusting in the Lord isn't knowing that those issues will no longer exist but that you are *choosing* the good portion. And in the next moment, when another trouble pesters you, you get to choose again. And again. And again.

Christ continues in Luke 10:42: *Which will not be taken away from her.* Christ is asking Martha to take a huge risk by putting down the shield of her well-received hard work and self-sufficient ministry. He is asking a lot of her fearful and prideful heart to sit down and listen alongside Mary, the one deemed unhelpful.

He knows something Martha doesn't. He knows that her worries and troubles will never go away. However hard she may try for good favor and however much she attains it, it will fade. However, Christ's love for Martha is everlasting. In the small things and in the big things, His love and wisdom are what she needs.

Christ wasn't just teaching Martha something for that moment, though. He encouraged a holy habit of trust because He was preparing Martha for what came next. He knew that she would need to strengthen her muscles of trust and surrender for the part she was to play in The Story. In these small worries and outcomes, He invited Martha to trust so that when impossibly hard days came along, she would have a habit of sitting in the Lord's care rather than hustling to earn His favor.

Let's look at John 11, later in the timeline of Mary and Martha.

We see Mary and Martha again, this time after their brother has died. Martha goes out to meet Jesus, but Mary stays back. We see even now how the tables have turned. Now, instead of the little worries like bread and broken tables, Martha has big things on her heart. She is heavy with grief, but her response is vastly different than before. This time she comes to Christ. She abandons the house of people gathered, people she's supposed to host, and runs to Christ. She leaves the control she thought she had and declares Christ as Lord.

"Martha said to Jesus, "Lord, if you had been here, my brother would not have died. But even now I know that whatever you ask from God, God will give you."

Jesus said to her, "Your brother will rise again."

Martha said to him, "I know that he will rise again in the resurrection on the last day."

Jesus said to her, "I am the resurrection and the life. Whoever believes in me, though he die, yet shall he live, and everyone who lives and believes in me shall never die. Do you believe this?"

She said to him, "Yes, Lord; I believe that you are the Christ, the Son of God, who is coming into the world. (John 11:20-27).

The practice of prioritizing and trusting Jesus is the only way we can prepare for the unexpected griefs of life. Christ didn't tell Martha to sit in Luke 10 because she needed a break. He invited her to sit because it would build up her muscles of trust to handle the death of her brother in John 11.

I love seeing the growth of Martha in these two stories. She goes from complaining about her sister to declaring faith in Christ even though her brother has died. She goes from trying to impress the Lord with her service to believing Him when it's hard. She practiced trusting God with the small things, which paved the way for the big ones.

PRACTICING TRUST

However much we think we can control the small parts of our lives and trust the Lord when the big things come our way, trust is a practice. It is a muscle, and just like our physical muscles, it needs to be strengthened through regular, rather mundane practice. Additionally, when our hands are busy holding up all of the little worries that we think we should be able to handle, they aren't ready to receive the dreams, work, and discipline of the kingdom.

Paul, when writing to Timothy, says, "Train yourself for godliness; for while bodily training is of some value, godliness is of value in every way, as it holds promise for the present life and also for the life to come. The saying is trustworthy and deserving of full acceptance" (1 Tim. 4:7-9).

Training for godliness isn't just showing up on gameday, and we all know this. I don't need to tell you that athletes train for the big day. Why would we think trusting the Lord is any different? Sometimes I fear that we think we can show up on the gameday of life, when big things are happening, and wing it with our trust.

This is not how it works. Building our trust muscle takes repetitive, consistent practice in the small things of life. We get so many opportunities to strengthen it if we keep our eyes open. Sometimes this is the boring kind of trust, trust that helps you not to speed through the traffic because you're late. Sometimes this is hard, ordinary trust like not stopping in front of the mirror to be insecure about your stretch marks. Sometimes it is the regular sort of trust, like spending time with Jesus when the dishes aren't finished yet.

My challenge to you, as we wrap up this book, is to figure out how we can change the *daily* narratives of our minds to trust the Lord. How can we tell a different story than the one the world tells? How can we take all of the little ways that we trust ourselves, circumstances, or others, and direct that trust to the Lord? How can we take our big dreams, like writing a book, or our little dreams, like taking a real day off, and trust them in the hands of the Father? How can we take our big disappointments, like a breakup, or our daily disappointments, like work being difficult, and walk in faith, not by sight? How can we take our big disasters, like a hurricane, or our little disasters, like forgetting about a deadline, and know that God is working in all things? Nothing is too big, but nothing is too small, either.

* * *

My original plan for the ending of this chapter was a list of practical steps to help nourish a holy habit of trust. I like that list. I think it's helpful and true. But after spending time with Martha, I wonder if the list is necessary or if we would take it and try to impress the Lord with our ability to trust. I wonder if we need a list or if we really just need *one thing*.

So instead of a list, I give you the One Thing.

Sit with Jesus. Make that your holy habit. When there are five things unchecked on your list at the end of the day, choose to trust Him enough to spend time with Him. When your spouse is acting strange and you want to fix the situation immediately, talk with Him. When you are overwhelmed, under-cared-for, and lonely, choose to praise Him. For we get a choice. We are not victims to hustle or to anxieties. Choose to cast your anxieties into the ocean of His care (1 Pet 5:7).

From that posture, I know that all these things will be given to us as well, (Matt. 6:33) for He spares no spiritual blessing (Eph. 1:3). From sitting with the

Lord, we receive a vibrant prayer life, which we need to trust the Lord. From sitting with the Lord, we receive a convicted heart, which we need to move forward in faith. From sitting with the Lord, we receive wisdom in seeking others who sit with the Lord for counsel, which we need to grow in the church. From with the Lord, we receive clarity, energy, and assurance to do the work in front of us to do.

But first, we sit.

We know that we have no control, even over the little things. First we make it our habit to declare Christ as Lord and ourselves as not-Lord. Then we can *know* and *rest* in the knowledge that the peace, care, and assurance that flows from Christ to our little hearts will not be taken away.

GROWING ROOTS

- ▶ Do you trust the Lord with your stretch marks (or other small areas of struggle)?
- ▶ What is making you worried and upset?
- ▶ How will you sit down at the feet of Jesus today? What about tomorrow?

CHAPTER TWELVE

Patterned Trust

The Psalms as an
Illustration of How We Change
the Narrative of our Minds

The turns you make to come home
Replying "you too"
Locking the door
Reaching for their hand
Making coffee
Warming up for a workout
Signing your name
Brushing your teeth

Do not discredit the value of
muscle memory
and the beaten path of our lives—
but may our muscle memory
memorize Christ
in a thousand little ways.

I am a verse and word of the year kind of gal, and in 2021, my verses were in Psalm 37 and my word was "delight." Almost two years later, that psalm is still the most visited place in my Bible, and I pay attention every time someone says "delight." This psalm has truly reoriented my heart during some beautiful and some rough seasons. It has taught my soul new words to say when anxiety and fear crept in.

The way I do verse of the year is that when I don't know where to turn, I turn there. When I don't know how to handle life, I turn to my verse of the year. I let it ground the year and teach my soul kingdom values over and over again. (I would highly recommend praying over a verse and word of the year. You don't have to be ultra-spiritual about it. Just be sensitive to what the Lord is teaching you and pick an area to grow in for the year or season. It's not only a helpful way to grow, but it helps me to remember, years down the road, what the Lord taught me each year.)

I want to teach my heart and yours the same thing when we want to grab tightly to our dreams, expectations, and disappointments. I want to train my soul and yours to tell a new narrative when life goes in an unexpected, different direction or when our hopes take their time to come about. I adore the Psalms because they help me do that. They take all of those fears, emotions, hopes, and situations and change them into praise.

Our hearts tell us a narrative all the time, and the untrusting heart tells a compelling story. Our anxious hearts tell us that we are behind, we are alone, and we are crippled. The lies of Satan want to make us the victim of our circumstances and keep us stuck in the pit of a pity party. Without vigilant watch, we easily spiral into self-centered, outcome-, answer-, or feeling-based narratives that increase our view of self and limit our view of God. We've already walked through the shortcomings of each of those thoughts.

The Psalms teach us a new narrative for our troubled souls, one of exalting the Lord, thanking His provision, hoping in His promises, and clinging to His character. They don't sugar-coat the pain of life or the disappointments that we face, but they look instead to the glory, the care, and the hope of the Lord. The Psalms are places where we can sit down with all our struggles and know the Lord *here.*

We've already unpacked many truths from the Psalms in this journey, but let's go through Psalm 37 today and learn from it how to rewrite the story we tell ourselves in our thoughts and prayer lives. We won't look at each verse in these pages, but please take the time now to read the entire psalm. We'll look at some broad themes and then a few key verses.

Seriously, don't read any more of this book until you read Psalm 37. All forty beautiful verses.

Okay, now that you're back, we can go forward.

The psalm comes from a place where David stood at the crossroads of desire and disappointment. The wicked are prospering, and he is left empty-handed. The way of the unrighteous seems to be going better. Has God forsaken him? The psalm is a war-cry for the anxious heart, filled with short, direct commands for us and sure, strong responses from God. It resembles a proverb in its structure, but it holds the struggle and feelings of the psalms. There are many psalms dealing with anxious hearts, but I find this one different than most because it is tactical and comforting at the same time. The entire psalm is filled with *active trust.*

"Fret not" (Ps. 37:1, 7, 8). "Trust in the LORD" (37:3, 5). "Delight yourself in the Lord" (37:4). "Commit your ways to the LORD" (37:5). "Be still before the LORD" (37:7). "Wait for the LORD" (37:34). "Take refuge in him" (37:40).

These are all postures of active trust. They aren't actions that fix unrighteousness or solve our issues. They are placing those issues in the hands of God. They are opening our hands around our fears, frustrations, and failures. They are verbalizing the simple, hard paths that the Psalmist chooses to take. They are a new role for us to play in the narrative, one not of the savior but of the saved, not one of the competent but one of the reliant. They are instructing our hearts to see the Lord at work, and then (here's the fun part) the Psalmist details what the work of the Lord is:

"He will give you the desires of your heart" (Ps. 37:4). "He will act" (37:5) "He will bring forth your righteousness" (37:6). "The LORD laughs at the wicked" (37:13). "The LORD upholds the righteous" (37:17). "The LORD knows the days of the blameless" (37:18). "The steps of man are established by the LORD" (37:23). "The LORD upholds his hand" (37:24). "The LORD loves justice" (37:28). "He will not forsake his saints" (37:28). "The LORD will not abandon him" (37:33). "He will exalt you" (37:34). "He is their stronghold" (37:39). "The LORD helps them and delivers them; he delivers then from the wicked and saves them" (37:40).

I don't know about you, but reading all the responses of God back-to-back like this gets me *excited*! Oh, how capable He is. Oh, how good He is. Oh, how marvelous are His works! Oh, how tender is His care! These words surround my anxious soul and put me in my place, under the mighty hand of God.

What God's Word tells us here is to take our fears, anxieties, and reluctance to trust in tow and to then take refuge in the God who delivers. We don't manage the outcomes or have the grand actions for the battle; we simply live under the wings of the Lord, trusting Him to win the war and fight our battles. We, in that shadow, get to do our part, get to do good, and get to pursue justice. Our actions do not win the war, God's do. And He will act. It says so right here. **He will act.**

Let's go through a few stanzas of this psalm and further instruct our souls on how to reorient around the Lord's ways.

The most famous part of this psalm, and what originally captivated me, is verses 3-4.

TRUSTING WITH OUR DESIRES

> Trust in the LORD, and do good; dwell in the land and befriend faithfulness. Delight yourself in the LORD, and he will give you the desires of your heart.
>
> —PSALM 37:3-4

This book is about trusting the Lord, right? Notice how David tells his soul to trust the Lord: Do good. Be where you are. Continue in faithfulness. Delight in the Lord. We tend to skip to the "he will give you the desires of your heart" part, but it is the last part of these two verses. First comes trust, doing good, dwelling where you are, and choosing faithfulness. The result is delighting in the Lord, and *then* comes the desires of our hearts. This is that habitual trust that we just talked about. This is the daily choice to spend time with Jesus even if the dishes aren't finished.

I see two ways to interpret Psalm 37:4. Either delighting in the Lord prepares our hearts to receive His gracious provision of our desires, *or* delighting in the Lord *is* the desire of our hearts. I wrestled with these two interpretations for a minute (or rather, a year). I obviously didn't think that the Lord just hands out fulfilled dreams to all of his followers—just look at the prophets. But I also know that He is a good Father and longs to be gracious to us. I waited to see what the year would teach me.

So, in 2021, I dedicated myself to delighting in the Lord. My prayers were vibrant, I sought more community than ever before, and I reprioritized my time so that I could practice stillness. I read more books. I truly treasured the delight of the Lord in my heart and loved every moment of it. It was practice. It was work. It was discipline, but man, was it delightful.

Then, at the end of the year, the year dedicated to Psalm 37:4, the year of delight, the year of passion for the Lord, a godly man asked to pursue me. It made so much sense to me. One of the biggest desires of my heart is marriage, and it seemed as if my life might head that way after all. After spending all year delighting in Him, the Lord was giving me the desire of my heart. Right?

2022 told a different story.

In the wake of heartbreak, Psalm 37 was a different sort of comfort. When the Lord took away what I desired, what was I left with?

Delight.

Some days after the breakup, I wrote: "Perhaps delighting in the Lord didn't give me a love story with the perfect man, but it made me desire the love of a perfect God. You are the desire of my heart, Lord. I know you are all I will ever need. I will spend eternity puzzling out your love. I will be enamored forever with the riches of your care. I acknowledge that I also desire love of a man and marriage, but I have greater confidence in You than in that. You are the greatest desire of my heart. More than anything that You could do, I just want You."

The Lord didn't take away my desire for love, but He filled my heart with something greater. I can say *confidently* now that I know to delight in the Lord is my desire. The more I delight in Him, the more I desire to delight in Him. Being near to Christ changes the orientation of our hearts. Instead of wishing for outcomes, answers, and feelings, we long for the surpassing glory of the gospel. Being near to Christ changes our desires and makes them more like Christ, from one degree of glory to the next (from 2 Cor. 3:18, my 2022 verse of the year).

"When we enjoy God, not just his gifts, but God himself, then the desires of our heart are shaped, are defined and created, in accord with our delight in him... The reason those who delight themselves in the Lord receive the desires of their heart is not just because one causes the other, but because one shapes the other. Delighting in God supremely determines, shapes the kinds of desires that we have in our heart."[26]

Thus, we see already, in the first four verses of Psalm 37, how David is shaping his thoughts to be near to God and delight in His ways, even when disappointment lurks close. He *chooses* to walk in obedience and make the Lord His priority, and that is David's great delight. He is committed to this way and tells it to God.

---

26 John Piper, "Is Oprah Right on Psalm 37:4?" Desiring God, March 8, 2016, https://www.desiringgod.org/interviews/is-oprah-right-on-psalm-37-4.

TRUSTING WITH OUR DISAPPOINTMENTS

> Commit your way to the Lord; trust in him, and
> he will act. He will bring forth your righteousness
> as the light, and your justice as the noonday. . .
> . Be still before the Lord and wait patiently for
> him; fret not yourself over the one who prospers
> in his way, over the man who carries out evil
> devices . . . wait for the Lord and keep his way,
> and he will exalt you to inherit the land; you will
> look on when the wicked are cut off.
>
> —PSALM 37:5–7, 34

Remember right here that David is teaching his heart to trust the Lord, even when he sees undesirable things, even when evildoers are prospering and disappointment greets him at every turn. He isn't writing from a place of victory but a place of disappointments. Therefore, David instructs his anxious heart to sing a new narrative, and that narrative is to:

1. **Commit.** Commit to the Lord. It's 100 percent. We've talked about this, as you may remember. Just like Proverb 3:5, Psalm 37 doesn't do anything halfway. David is committed. He is pre-deciding to trust the Lord.

2. **Trust.** Give up your own understanding and know the Lord. Put all your chips and chipped pieces

on the table. David is rewriting the narrative of distrust and replacing it with the command for his soul to trust the Lord.

3. **Wait.** Even when you see others racing ahead, trust that God's plan for you will be glorious. He has an inheritance for you; you need only be still. God is never late, but He isn't always working according to your watch.

When disappointments come, our troubled souls and closing fingers want immediacy. Long suffering and unanswered questions tend to make us antsy and fidgety. Fidgety fingers often curl in around our plans. This is only worsened when others start to do laps around us. This psalm pits David's fate with those of the wicked, but we can even compare ourselves with the righteous. *Why does she get pregnant right away when I've waited years? How is it that she is healthy and eats whatever she wants when I have to be so careful with what I eat? Why does she get to get married when I can't even get a date?*

What does David do with those thoughts? He carefully redirects them to commit, trust, and wait. There is such power when we can use what the enemy intends for harm and redirect it for glory. Our anxious thoughts and disappointing circumstances do not define us if we pre-decide to point them to the hands of a faithful God.

Then, listen up folks, *the Lord will act.*

Trust in the Lord, and He will act. Commit your ways to the Lord, and He will act. He's working all the time, even now (John 5:17). He isn't taking His time; He's using it. He isn't dragging His feet; He's setting yours in secure places (Ps. 40:2). He isn't teasing you; He's testing your faith so that it will be like refined gold (1 Pet. 1:7).

In the story *right now,* we get to trust Him with open hands. In the waiting, we commit. In the disappointments, we trust. And you get to know *right here* and *right now,* that He is faithful, and He will do it (1 Thes. 5:24). We get to take Him at His word here. It is God who works in us to will and to act according to His good purposes (Phil. 2:13).

TRUSTING WITH OUR DISASTERS

The LORD knows the days of the blameless, and their heritage will remain forever; they are not put to shame in evil times; in the days of famine they have abundance . . . the steps of a man are established by the LORD, when he delights in his way; though he fall, he shall not be cast headlong, for the LORD upholds his hand . . . The salvation of the righteous is from the LORD; he is their stronghold in the time of trouble. The LORD helps them and delivers them; he delivers them from the wicked and saves them, because they take refuge in him.

—PSALM 37:18–19, 23–24, 39–40

David isn't talking about little bumps in the road in these verses. He is talking about evil times, famine, falling, trouble, and wickedness. He is talking about the disasters. He is talking about the moments where none of it makes sense. How does David take these real threats and questions and redirect his heart to trust God amidst disaster?

He knows that the Lord holds him. He knows that the Lord is strong for him. He knows that the Lord helps him, delivers him, and saves him. David puts his hope and praise in who God is, and that is David's foundation when disaster strikes.

There are three ways David processes the disasters in his life in these verses:

One, he doesn't deny them. David isn't all sunshine and rainbows. I wonder if we, as Christians, want to put on this "it's okay" face, even when it's not okay. We may look around and see that we *don't* have the healing, relationships, resources, or timelines that we want or need. Like David, recognize your need and suffering. Say them out loud to the Lord. Place them in your hands and let them take up space without disregarding them as trivial or unholy.

Two, he recognizes how the Lord works through disasters. Notice how David is never the rescuer in these verses. Famine leads to abundance from the Lord. David falls, but the Lord catches him. Times of trouble come, but the Lord is a stronghold. The Lord's provisions are front and center. The Lord isn't counting on us to respond perfectly to disasters, for we cannot. He is leading us to rely on Him in times of trouble. He is leading us to trust.

Three, he doesn't let disasters have the final word. David says that in the dry places, in the time of disaster and evil and disappointment, we are not put to shame. Whatever disaster you face right now is not the end of the story, and our little brains need to remember this. Illness is not the end of the story; healing is. Loneliness is not the end of the story; love is. Failure is not the end of the story; salvation is. If not on this side of heaven, then we will see these things on the other side of heaven. For the answers to the longings of our souls is a "yes" from Christ, only sometimes we receive these blessings in heaven rather than on Earth.

As David ends his war-cry of trust with a bang, he reminds himself who God is. The Lord is Savior, a stronghold, helper, deliverer, and refuge. And since that is who God is, David can be still and wait for the Lord to act according to who He is. The Lord then saves, protects, helps, delivers, and guards.

So, with this echoing in our hearts, we take refuge in Him. We hide in the shelter of His wings (Ps. 91:4), a safe place to keep our hands open. When the lies of the world, the pressures of our expectations, and the disappointments of our circumstances narrow in on us, we take shelter in the wings of God and find space there. In the shelter of who God is, we can trust, wait, commit, and delight. We take Him at His Word. We change the narrative of our minds to glorify the Lord. We dwell there in safety and awe, a strange mix of emotions only accomplished through grace.

But the first step, the step I encourage you to take today as we wrap up this book, is this: pre-decide to trust. Take your mind and bend it to trust. Dedicate your study and prayers to trust. Exercise your faith and dependency upon God. It takes practice. God knows I'm not there yet either. This book was a huge reminder for me to continue to work on keeping my plans in open hands. But with these encouragements from His Word and His character, we are enabled and equipped to live the open-handed life.

My friend, the open-handed life waits for us. God beckons to us. Let us go.

GROWING ROOTS

▶ What tools have you learned to trust the Lord with your desires?

▶ How can you redirect your thoughts when there are disappointments?

▶ What is our hope in disasters?

CLOSING

The funny thing about writing this book is that I didn't mean to write it. Most of this manuscript was me puzzling out my thoughts on how to trust God with a particular set of trials in my life. I thought it was a blog post series *maybe,* but certainly not a book. So, I just wrote. And wrote. Every night I came to these pages from 11 p.m. to 1 a.m. I can only attribute this season of fervent writing and listening (and not sleeping) to the Lord. In two months, I had the longest blog post no one would read.

What I didn't know was that I needed this more than anyone else.

In the original writing process, I held some specific desires. I wanted the boy back. I wanted my ankle healed. I wanted my job to work out. Over the next year I watched the boy marry a different girl. My ankle continues to give me problems. I love my job, though, so not all things are hard.

The entire writing process tested the firmness of my theme. I learned and continued to learn the hard way to hold those plans in open hands. I learned to let go of some dreams and follow after others. I was far less affected by disappointments that came my way. I felt so rooted in the Lord's provision that even some strange worst-case scenarios felt . . . okay.

This isn't even mentioning how the steps of publishing a book required some open-handedness. It was one thing to write out all my thoughts every night when I had very little going on. It's another thing entirely to stay up editing and deciding on book covers after working twelve-hour days.

I look back and see so much fruit from keeping my plans in open hands. I have tested and approved that the insights and wisdoms in this book, all pulled from the Word, are beneficial, reliable, and life changing. They withstood quite a few tests in my life.

I look forward and see much hope in keeping my plans in open hands. My prayer is that these words, these stories, and the Word of God encourage your heart to trust God more and more. My confidence is that you, too, will be able to look back and see the fruit in your life of keeping your plans in open hands. Let it be your mantra. Let it be your rhythm. Let it be your posture.

It is worth it, my friends, I have seen it so clearly. He is worth it.

Together, let's keep our plans in open hands *to the Lord.*

ACKNOWLEDGEMENTS

Writing a book is far more isolating than I anticipated, yet this work could not have been completed without the help of these wonderful people.

My family listened to hours of brainstorming and sorting out my thoughts. Thank you Mom, Dad, Rebecca, Abigail, and Elisabeth for being a safe space to grow. Y'all are my first and biggest cheerleaders. I'll never forget that hike in Colorado when my Daddy told me to go for it and I decided to publish this little book. Thank you Daddy, for hyping me up along the way. Thank you Mom for being my rock, Grammar Police, and friend. Thank you Rebecca for being protective over my heart. Thank you Elisabeth for your wisdom. Thank you Abigail for looking like a fool with me while taking pictures of my hands at the park.

My friends have been so insightful and encouraging! Thank you for your many conversations about trusting the Lord and support with the publishing process. Y'all are my spring pad from which to launch, and I'm excited to share this with you.

The staff and support from hope*writers was God-sent. It was no accident that one week after I completed these thoughts, I got an email about a new publishing company. Brian, Krissy, Abby, and the rest of the team made these words into a book during a hectic season of my life.

Obviously the MVP is Jesus Christ. But if you've made it this far, you already know that.